BLENDER 2025 FOR BEGINNERS & EXPERTS: THE ULTIMATE GUIDE TO 3D MODELING, ANIMATION, RENDERING & VFX

UNLOCK CUTTING-EDGE FEATURES WITH STEP-BY-STEP TUTORIALS, ADVANCED TECHNIQUES, AND INDUSTRY-PROVEN WORKFLOWS FOR STUNNING VISUAL CREATIONS

ROBBIE NICKSON

TABLE OF CONTENTS

CHAPTER 1

OVERVIEW OF BLENDER (VERSION 4.3- 4.4)

Unleash Your Creativity: Master 3D with Blender 2025

Imagine having a single, **powerful, free, and open-source** tool that lets you create stunning 3D animations, breathtaking visual effects, hyper-realistic game assets, and cinematic-quality films—all without spending a fortune on software licenses. **Welcome to Blender 2025 (Version 4.4), the ultimate all-in-one 3D creation suite.**

Whether you're a **beginner exploring the world of 3D,** a **professional seeking a robust alternative to expensive software,** or a **studio looking for an efficient, scalable workflow,** this guide is designed to help you **unlock the full potential of Blender**—no matter your skill level.

Blender 2025 is more than just a tool; it's a **game-changer in the world of digital content creation.** With its ever-evolving features, industry-grade capabilities, and **a thriving global community**, it stands tall as one of the most versatile and widely used 3D software applications today.

This guide is your roadmap to mastering Blender 2025, helping you:

✓ Navigate Blender's interface and tools effortlessly

✓ Create high-quality 3D models, animations, and visual effects

✓ Optimize workflows for better efficiency and faster results

✓ Understand the principles of 3D design, rendering, and simulation

✓ Turn your creative ideas into professional-grade projects

No matter where you are in your **3D journey**, this user guide will equip you with the **knowledge, techniques, and insider tips** needed to take full advantage of Blender's capabilities.

What Makes Blender 2025 Stand Out?

Blender 2025 (Version 4.4) isn't just another 3D software—it is a **feature-packed, open-source powerhouse** that competes with top-tier paid alternatives. Here's why it stands out:

1. A Fully Integrated 3D Creation Suite

Blender provides a **complete** 3D production pipeline, covering:

- **Modeling & Sculpting** – Advanced tools for hard surface modeling and organic sculpting.

Animation & Rigging – A professional-grade animation system with powerful rigging capabilities.

- **Rendering** – Real-time and high-quality rendering powered by **Cycles** and **Eevee**.
- **Video Editing** – A built-in **Non-Linear Editor (NLE)** for editing and compositing.
- **VFX & Motion Tracking** – Industry-standard tools for professional-level visual effects.
- **Compositing & Post-Processing** – Node-based compositing for seamless post-production.
- **Simulation & Physics** – Realistic cloth, fire, smoke, water, and soft-body simulations.

2. Cross-Platform Compatibility

Blender runs seamlessly on **Windows, macOS, and Linux**, offering:

- **A consistent OpenGL-powered interface** across all platforms.
- **Customizable UI and workflow adaptation** using Python scripting.
- **A fully portable setup,** allowing Blender to run from any directory without system modifications.

3. High-Performance & Optimized Workflow

- **Multi-threaded processing** and **GPU acceleration** for faster rendering.
- **Optimized viewport performance,** enabling smooth real-time interactions.
- **A modular and non-destructive workflow,** allowing for creative flexibility.

3

4. Free & Open-Source with a Massive Community

- **No licensing fees or subscription costs**—Blender is completely free for personal and commercial use.
- **An ever-growing, passionate community** of artists, developers, and studios continuously improving the software.
- **Extensive learning resources,** including tutorials, forums, and documentation.

Who Uses Blender?

Blender's power and versatility make it an essential tool for:

✓ **Animation Studios & Filmmakers** – Producing professional 3D animated films and VFX sequences.

✓ **Game Developers** – Designing game-ready assets, characters, and environments.

✓ **Architects & Designers** – Creating detailed architectural visualizations and product prototypes.

✓ **Motion Graphic Artists** – Crafting engaging visual effects, title sequences, and branding content.

✓ **Content Creators & YouTubers** – Editing videos, designing intros, and enhancing multimedia content.

✓ **3D Printing Enthusiasts** – Designing and refining models for real-world 3D printing.

Blender is used by **both beginners and industry professionals**, proving its ability to cater to a wide range of creative needs. Whether you're just starting out or looking to **level up your skills,** Blender has the tools and flexibility to help you bring your ideas to life.

How This Guide Will Help You Master Blender 2025

Learning Blender may seem overwhelming at first, given its vast array of tools and functionalities. However, this guide is designed to **simplify your learning curve** by providing:

✅ **Step-by-step instructions** – Making complex tasks easy to follow and execute.

✅ **Real-world examples and practical exercises** – Helping you apply what you learn immediately.

✅ **Clear explanations of technical concepts** – Breaking down 3D jargon into simple terms.

☑ **Time-saving tips and shortcuts** – Boosting your efficiency and productivity.

☑ **Best practices from industry experts** – Ensuring you develop professional-level skills.

By the end of this guide, you will be **confidently navigating Blender, creating high-quality 3D models and animations,** and **optimizing your workflow for maximum efficiency.**

Mastering the Art of 3D Creation

Blender is an incredible tool, but like any creative software, **it's only as powerful as the artist behind it**. Great 3D art isn't just about using the right tools—it's about mastering **composition, lighting, animation principles, and storytelling**.

Take the time to **practice, experiment, and explore.** The more you engage with Blender, the more you'll **unlock its full potential** and push the boundaries of what's possible.

So, let's get started. **Your 3D journey begins now!**

CHAPTER 2

EXPLORING THE EVOLUTION OF BLENDER

~~The Innovation from Humble Starts to Global Dominance~~

Blender's open-source journey has been marked by rapid innovation owing to its particular model of development. Unlike other software firms with rigid corporate hierarchies, Blender thrives through collaboration between full-time developers, volunteers, and hobbyist users around the world. The distributed model facilitates rapid cycles of iteration, tuning, and inclusion of sophisticated features.

One of the largest accomplishments of Blender was the integration of the **Cycles render engine** into version 2.61 (2011). Cycles revolutionized the world of rendering for Blender with a **path-tracing engine** that featured realistic lighting, shadows, and materials. It has since added **AMD and NVIDIA GPU support, adaptive subdivision, volumetrics, and advanced shaders.**

The **2.8 release in 2019** was another landmark. Prior to that, Blender couldn't achieve any industry recognition because the majority of professionals saw it as a tool for hobbyists and not an alternative to proprietorial tools like Autodesk Maya or 3ds Max. With the release of 2.8, perceptions changed. With **a reworked user interface, the introduction of EEVEE (an extremely powerful real-time**

rendering engine), a new dependency graph, and enhanced sculpting tools, Blender was a direct challenger to be used by large animation houses, game studios, and VFX artists. This innovation in capability generated **unrivaled industry attention**. Large companies, such as **Ubisoft, Epic Games, NVIDIA, AMD, and Microsoft,** started financially sponsoring Blender via the **Blender Development Fund.** This money enabled Blender's development to increase at a rate that allowed it to directly compete with high-end proprietary software yet remain entirely free for everyone.

Blender Cloud and Open Projects

To help its users even more, the **Blender Cloud** was launched—a subscription website with training, assets, and access to the behind-the-scenes on Blender's Open Projects. It's both a learning tool and library of **excellent-quality assets, production files, animation breakdowns, and shaders**, where users can learn from seeing how the pros work.

Blender's **Open Movies** continue to push its limits. Each project is a stress test of what Blender can do, and each finds areas for improvement. Short films made by the **Blender Studio** have enabled new features such as complex hair simulation, improved character animation tools, and new rendering methods.

Some of the most well-known Open Movies are:

- **Elephants Dream (2005)** – Blender's first Open Movie, showcasing procedural animation and detailed environments.
- **Big Buck Bunny (2008)** – A comedic animation that added to Blender's fur, grass, and high-definition texture capabilities.

- **Sintel (2010)** – A darker, emotion-based story that added to Blender's character animation and storytelling capabilities.
- **Tears of Steel (2012)** – A sci-fi film that introduced high-end **motion tracking and VFX compositing** into Blender.
- **Sprite Fright (2021)** – A horror comedy that focused on improving Blender's **Grease Pencil and NPR (non-photorealistic rendering) tools.**

These films not only improve Blender but are also a testament to what is possible with **free and open-source software.**

The Current Scenario: Blender's Place in the Industry

Blender is no longer a specialized tool today—it is a **mainstream 3D creation suite** used by industry professionals across the board. **Film studios, game developers, architects, and visual effects professionals** now have Blender as part of their workflows. The use of **real-time engines like Unreal Engine and Unity** has also boosted Blender's status, as it exports directly to these platforms.

Blender is now widely used in:

- **Game Development** – Blender is used by indie and AAA game development studios for modeling, texturing, and animation.
- **Visual Effects (VFX)** – Motion tracking, compositing, and simulation tools of Blender are used in film and television production.

- **Architecture & Product Design** – Architects and industrial designers use Blender's precise modeling and rendering capabilities.
- **Virtual Reality (VR) & Augmented Reality (AR)** – Blender is used to create assets for immersive experiences.
- Blender's capability to support **AI workflows, procedural modeling, and advanced physics simulations continues to expand, positioning it as a force to be reckoned with for digital artists, engineers, and scientists** as well.

The Future: Where is Blender Headed?

Blender's roadmap is aggressive. With increasing financial support, the Blender Foundation is striving to increase its core team, reduce development cycles, and improve user experience. Some of the primary areas of concentration include:

1. Performance Improvements

- **Faster rendering with Cycles X,** improving GPU acceleration and real-time ray tracing.
- **Improved viewport performance,** allowing artists to work on higher-poly models without lag.

2. Next-Generation Animation & Rigging Tools

- Blender will **compete with Autodesk Maya** by simplifying its rigging, skinning, and character animation workflows.
- Animation layers, enhanced motion paths, and real-time physics interaction will solidify Blender's place in professional pipelines even more.

3. Procedural Workflows & Geometry Nodes

- **Blender's Geometry Nodes system** is evolving to enable procedural modeling, similar to Houdini.
- Artists will be able to create **fully procedural landscapes, cities, and effects** with node-based systems.

4. AI & Machine Learning Integration

- AI-based **denoising, auto-rigging, and real-time texture upscaling** will be forecast to enhance Blender's toolset.
- Machine learning-driven **facial animation and motion capture software** could make Blender a leading product for film and game creation.

5. Virtual & Augmented Reality Support

- **Native VR sculpting and modeling tools** will allow artists to create within virtual worlds.
- **Augmented reality asset creation** will be more embedded, opening up new interactive media possibilities.

Blender's Mission: Open-Source for Everyone

Despite its enormous success, Blender is **still committed to its original mission:**

"Get the world's best 3D technology into the hands of artists as open-source, and make amazing things with it.".

This philosophy ensures that Blender will **never be paywalled** or owned by a corporation. The Blender Foundation remains committed to **freedom, innovation, and community development,** ensuring that Blender is not just a tool, but a movement.

The history of Blender is one of perseverance, ingenuity, and open-source teamwork. From a lowly origin as a tiny in-house tool at NeoGeo to industry-leading 3D software, development of Blender has been motivated by **dedicated developers, artists, and contributors from all around the world.**

With its ever-expanding features, industry adoption, and unwavering open-source philosophy, Blender is poised to remain at the forefront of 3D content creation for decades to come. Whether you're a beginner experimenting with your first model or a professional artist working on a blockbuster film, Blender offers limitless possibilities—completely free.

With technology continuing to evolve, there is one certainty: **Blender is here to stay, shaping the future of 3D creation and holding fast to its roots of accessibility, innovation, and open-source development.**

The Start: A Dream Takes Shape (1994 – 2001)

Blender's origin dates back to **January 1994**, in the premises of the Dutch animation studio **NeoGeo**, where it was first born. Over the next few years, it spread incrementally, incorporating support for other platforms like **SGI (1998), Linux, FreeBSD, Sun, and Linux Alpha.** By **November 1998,** Blender released its **very first manual**, a turning point in its journey.

In **April 1999**, there was a new licensing scheme introduced—users could unlock more features using a **C-Key,** which would be **$95**. But by **June 2000**, Blender fully embraced its open philosophy, abolishing the C-Key and fully opening the software to **freeware.**

Blender continued to develop even more rapidly, incorporating an **interactive 3D and real-time engine (2000)** and a **new physics engine with Python support (2000-2001).** Incorporating **character animation tools (2001)** made it a serious contender in the 3D market.

Going Open Source: A Bold Leap (2002 – 2003)

The greatest moment of transformation occurred on **October 13, 2002**, when Blender was **Officially Open Source,** a milestone celebrated by partying at the very first **Blender Conference.** This was followed by the free availability of the **Blender Publisher,** which set the stage for later explosive community growth.
It was in **2003** that Blender had enormous UI designing as well as new rendering features, including **ambient occlusion** and **new procedural textures.**

The 2.x Period: Expansion & Innovation (2004 – 2015)

Blender during this period became a software standard in the industry:
- **2004-2005:** New modeling tools added, UV mapping enhanced, soft bodies, force fields, and multi-threaded rendering.
- **2006-2007: Nodes introduced,** with increased physics, multi-pass rendering, and subsurface scattering for real-world materials.

- **2008-2009**: Great advancements in particle systems, hair, fur, and sculpting tools. **Blender Game Engine (GE)** was also enhanced.

From **2009 to 2011**, the **Blender 2.5 series** completely redesigned the software, introducing a **new Python API**, an improved window manager, and a new UI. This was one of the biggest reworkings of Blender's history.

The subsequent years brought more stability and shine:

- **2011-2016:** The **Cycles renderer** was added (2011), and there were enhancements in motion tracking, fluid simulations, and sculpting. Dynamic topology, rigid body physics, and viewport rendering capabilities made it revolutionary.

The 2.8 Revolution: A New Age Begins (2019 – 2021)

In **July 2019,** Blender **2.80** launched a **massively rewritten UI** in the cause of a friendlier experience. The show-stopper was **EEVEE,** a harsh real-time rendering engine that brought Blender's workflow revolutionary. In addition to some of the big developments were:
- **Grease Pencil** evolved to be a 2D full animation system.
- **Collections** abandoned regular layers in favor of even more order.
- **Cycles, modeling, animation, and import/export utilities** received significantly upgraded.

The development team of Blender continued to develop the software with **2.81 - 2.93 LTS,** adding features like:

- **Cycles X** to accelerate rendering.

- **Advanced sculpting and animation tools.**
- **Virtual reality (VR) support for inspecting 3D scenes.**
- **A new asset browser for workflow optimization.**

Blender 3.x: The Next Level (2021 – Present)

By **December 2021, Blender 3.0** was released, bringing in:
- **A next-gen rendering engine (Cycles X).**
- **New Geometry Nodes** for advanced procedural modeling.
- **An improved pose library for character animation.**
- **Grease Pencil Line Art enhancements** for stylized rendering.

This was a new era focused on **performance optimization, usability, and AI features**, making Blender the leader as a 3D professional tool across the world.

Blender 3.0 – Optimized Performance

- **3.0 – December 2021:** Huge performance boost with the **Asset Browser, Cycles X** as a high-performance calculation completion, **EEVEE Attributes** as the new set of features to check EEVEE properties of a model, extended **Geometry Nodes,** Animation World Performance optimizations, an improvement in the **Grease Pencil Line Art**, a new **Pose Library** and optimized **Open Image Denoising** to the factor 8 faster performance.

- **3.1 – March 2022:** Some incredible improvements in **Geometry Nodes** with over **100 new nodes,** faster rendering on **Cycles X,** macOS support for **Metal GPU rendering,** improved **VR scene inspection,** and overall **performance and memory improvements.**

- **3.2 – June 2022:** The introduction of **Light Groups** in Cycles, a new **Shadow Caustics** system, painting in **Sculpt Mode, Grease Pencil** improvements, a **more efficient rendering pipeline,** and additional workflow and UI improvements.

- **3.3 LTS – September 2022:** A long-term support (LTS) release with significant additions like **Procedural UV Unwrapping in Geometry Nodes,** Intel® **Open Image Denoiser** enhancements, improved **Grease Pencil layers,** and an **accelerated, more responsive viewport.**

Blender 3.4 – Extending Capabilities

- **3.4 – December 2022:** Introduced the **Path Guiding Algorithm** for more realistic light behavior in Cycles, the **UV Unwrapping Packing Algorithm,** enhancements to **Geometry Nodes,** a new **Grease Pencil Fill tool, color space enhancements,** and overall performance enhancements.

- **3.5 – March 2023:** A **game-changer for hair grooming** with the **new Hair Curves system,** further improvements in **Geometry Nodes, Cycles optimizations,** and **animation workflows enhancements.**

- **3.6 LTS – June 2023:** Another long-term support release focused on **performance, stability, and new features,** including an **enhanced viewport experience,** improved **rigging tools, expanded simulation** capabilities, and **more complete Python API support** for advanced scripting.

Blender 4.0 – The Future of 3D Creation

- **4.0 – November 2023:** A landmark release with a **completely reworked rendering system**, major overhaul of **Geometry Nodes**, an **advanced shader framework, improvements in real-time viewport rendering,** and more **Grease Pencil features.**

- **4.1 – March 2024**: **AI-based modeling tools,** enhanced **real-time rendering**, a **new physics simulation system**, and further development of **animation and rigging.**

- **Blender 4.2 LTS – July 2024**

The **first Long-Term Support (LTS) release of the 4.x series,** Blender 4.2 LTS features a **massive revamp to EEVEE,** advancements in **Cycles,** and **workflow improvements** for both artists and developers.

Key Features & Improvements:

- **Next-Gen EEVEE**: Large improvements in **lighting, sun lights, displacement, subsurface scattering, volumetrics, and motion blur,** bringing real-time rendering closer to path-traced realism.
- **Cycles Enhancements:**
  - **Ray Portal BSDF** – Simplified light path tracing for improved indoor lighting fidelity.
  - **Thin-Film Interference** – Replicates iridescent materials like soap bubbles and oil slicks.
  - **Improved Soft Volume Rendering** – Reduces noise in fog, smoke, and cloud rendering.

- **Blue Noise-Based Sampling** – Enhances sampling efficiency, reducing render times.
- **Blender Extensions Platform Released** – A unified platform for managing add-ons and extensions.
- **Khronos PBR Neutral Tone Mapper** – Ensures accurate and consistent color representation on any platform.
- **Sculpting & Selection Upgrades:** Brush selection made more accessible and Node input matrices support for intricate shader pipelines.
- **Node Tools Upgrades:** Now with mouse position tracking and viewport-based interactions.
- **Video Sequencer Rewrite:** New UI and performance enhancements for smoother video editing.
- **More USD Export Options** – Enhanced interoperability with 3D workflows utilized in industries.
- **Native Portable Installation Support** – More comfortable to use across different devices without the need to install it.

Why Blender 4.2 LTS Matters

This LTS version **firmly establishes Blender 4.0's foundation**, offering long-term stability with cutting-edge rendering and workflow enhancements. It's crafted for artists, developers, and studios in need of a **stable, high-performance** set of 3D tools.

- **Blender 4.3 – November 2024**

Blender 4.3 **improves EEVEE's lighting system**, introduce **new procedural textures**, and **give new life to the Grease Pencil engine** for 2D/3D animation to a whole new level.

Key Features & Enhancements:

- **EEVEE Enhancements:**
  - **Light Linking & Shadow Linking** – Allowing artists to **correctly control which objects are affected by specific lights and shadows.**

- **Metallic BSDF Shader** – Provides more realistic metal surfaces.
  - **Gabor Noise Texture** – Provides more advanced, procedural noise texture for shaders.
  - **EEVEE Render Passes in the Compositor** – More post-processing control over **separate lighting and shading components.**
  - **Minimum Stretch (SLIM) UV Unwrapping** – Provides more precise texture mapping by minimizing stretching.

- **Geometry Nodes Improvements:**
  - **For Each Zone Improvements** – Increases procedural modeling.
  - **Physics Nodes** – Enables **procedural simulations,** increasing the interactivity of physics.

- **Grease Pencil Overhaul:**
  - **Engine Fully Rewritten** – Drastically increases **performance and feature set** for animation and sketching.

- **Painting & Sculpting Improvements:**
  - **100+ Default Brushes Included** – Includes Blender's standard toolset for digital sculpting and texture painting.

- **User Interface Improvements:**
  - **UI Area Docking** – Improves workspace organization through ability to dock and customize UI panels.

Blender 4.3 – Pushing Creativity Further

This release focuses on **tuning creative pipelines,** improving **procedural and physics animation,** and **simplifying the real-time render experience.** The **Grease Pencil rewrite alone** is a revolution for 2D animators and artists!

The Future for Blender

Blender's **rapid development cycle** continues to push the limits of **3D creation, animation, and real-time rendering**. With the **4.x series,** artists can expect:

- ✅ Accelerated real-time rendering with EEVEE
- ✅ Procedural tools more advanced with Geometry Nodes
- ✅ More powerful physics-based simulations
- ✅ A new-generation Grease Pencil engine
- ✅ More industry-standard interoperability

Blender is **free, open-source, and at the bleeding-edge,** remaining the most accessible **high-end 3D tool** to developers, studios, and artists.

Installing Blender:

Blender is updated approximately **every three months,** ensuring users have access to the latest features and improvements. You can stay informed about these updates through the official **release notes**.

System Requirements

Blender is compatible with **Windows, macOS, and Linux**. Before installing, ensure that your system meets the **minimum and recommended requirements** for optimal performance.

- **Graphics Drivers:** It is crucial to keep your GPU drivers updated to prevent compatibility issues.
- **OpenGL Support:** Blender relies on OpenGL, so make sure your system fully supports it.
- **Additional Hardware:** If you plan to use **graphics tablets or 3D mice**, you'll find detailed setup instructions in the **Configuring Hardware** section.

Downloading Blender

Blender provides several versions, each catering to different needs. The best choice depends on whether you prioritize **stability** or access to the **latest features**. Here's an overview of the available options:

1. Stable Release (Recommended for Most Users)

- This is the **officially tested version**, released approximately **every three months**.
- It includes the **latest features** while ensuring **stability** without known regressions.

2. Long-Term Support (LTS) Version (For Professional and Studio Use)

- Designed for **long-term projects** that require a highly **stable** environment.
- **Supported for two years**, meaning no new features, API changes, or major improvements will be introduced.
- A new LTS version is released **once per year**.

3. Daily Builds (For Developers and Enthusiasts)

- Updated **daily** with the latest development changes.
- Not as thoroughly tested as the stable version, meaning some features may break.
- Ideal for those who want **early access** to upcoming features.

Building Blender from Source (For Advanced Users)

Blender's **source code** is freely available, allowing advanced users to compile their own versions. While not required for typical users, compiling Blender offers some advantages:

- Always access the **latest version** and updates.
- Explore **experimental branches** where new features are being developed.
- Customize Blender to meet **specific needs**.

If you choose to build Blender from source, detailed instructions are provided in the official documentation.

Installing Blender

The installation process is the same regardless of whether you choose the **Stable Release**, **LTS Version**, or **Daily Builds**. Follow the appropriate steps for your **operating system**.

Note: Blender **does not include an automatic update system**. When a new version is released, you will need to **manually update** by following the upgrade steps outlined in the next section.

This version makes the content **clearer, more structured, and engaging**, while maintaining all the necessary information. Let me know if you'd like any refinements!

Installing Blender on Linux

If you have not already done so, go to the **Downloading Blender** page to ensure your system meets the minimum requirements and to view the different available versions of Blender.

Installation Methods

1. Installing from Blender.org (Official Binary Installation)

This method ensures you are using the latest official version of Blender.

Steps:
1. Visit [Blender.org](https://www.blender.org/) and download the **Linux version** corresponding to your system architecture.
2. Extract the downloaded file to a location of your choice, such as `~/software` or `/usr/local/`.
3. Blender can be simply **run by double-clicking the executable** (`blender`).

Advantages:
Always up-to-date with the latest features.

Can have more than one version installed simultaneously.

Optional Configuration:

- **Add a Menu Entry & File Associations:** To simplify access to Blender, include it in your system application menu and link the `.blend` file extension to it.
- **Portable Installation:** If you desire a fully standalone installation, install Blender as a **portable installation.**

2. Installing from a Package Manager
Many **Linux distributions** have Blender available in their software repositories.

Installation Steps:
- **Debian/Ubuntu-based distributions:** ```bash sudo apt install blender ```
  - **- Fedora:** ```bash sudo dnf install blender ```
  - **Arch Linux (via Pacman):** ```bash sudo pacman -S blender```

Advantages:
☑ Integrates with your system's package manager, making updates easier.
☑ May provide extra system-wide optimizations.

Disadvantages:
✖ The package may be **outdated** with respect to official Blender releases.
✖ Some features, like **Cycles GPU rendering,** might not be included because of licensing limitations.

3. Installing from Snap (Recommended for Automatic Updates)
Snap is a **universal package manager** that will ensure that you have the latest Blender updates at all times.

Installation Steps:
1. Make sure Snap is installed on your system. If not, install it with: ```bash sudo apt install snapd```
2. Install Blender using Snap: ```bash snap install blender --classic ```

Advantages:
☑ **Automatic updates** – no need to download new versions manually.
☑ **Consistent across different Linux distributions.**

Launching Blender from the Terminal

If you rather launch Blender directly from the terminal, navigate to the installation folder and enter: ```bash ./blender```
Or, when installed with **Snap** or a package manager, you simply enter: ```bash blender```

Additional Linux-Specific Configuration

Avoiding Alt-Key Conflicts
Some **window managers** use `Alt + Left Mouse Button (LMB)` to move windows, which conflicts with Blender's hotkeys.

To fix this, **remap the window modifier key:**

For GNOME:
Run this command in the terminal: ```bash gsettings set org.gnome.desktop.wm.preferences mouse-button-modifier '<Super>'
```

(This will take effect after logging out and back in.)

**For KDE:**
Go to **System Settings** → **Window Management** → **Window Behavior** → **Window Actions** → Change `Alt` to `Meta` (Windows key).

## Updating Blender on Linux

### 1. Update Blender from Blender.org
- Get the new release from [Blender.org](https://www.blender.org/).
- Unpack and overwrite your existing installation using the same instructions in the **official binary installation** above.

### 2. Update using Package Manager
If you installed Blender using your Linux distribution's package manager, update it with:

- **Debian/Ubuntu:** ```bash sudo apt update && sudo apt upgrade blender``````
- **Fedora:** ```bash sudo dnf update blender ```
- **Arch Linux:** ```bash sudo pacman -Syu blender ```
```

3. Updating Snap Installation (Automatic Updates Enabled)

Updates are automatic if Blender was installed via Snap. However, updates can be forced manually with: ```bash snap refresh blender```

Known Limitations

Archive Extraction Issues

Blender's `.tar` file must be extracted using **TAR** and not 7-Zip. To extract it correctly, use: ```bash tar -xvf **blender-.tar.xz**```

This one makes the material **better organized, easier to read, and more interesting,** with all the technical stuff in there. If you would like some adjustments, let me know!

Installing Blender on macOS

Before you install Blender, visit the **Downloading Blender** page and check the **minimum system requirements** so that you can download the appropriate version for your **Mac's CPU architecture.**

Note: Blender is compatible with both **Intel-based Macs** and **Apple Silicon (M1, M2, M3, etc.)** Macs. Make sure to **download the appropriate version matching your CPU architecture.**

Installation Steps (DMG File)

Blender for macOS comes in the form of a **DMG (disk image) file**. To install it, follow these steps:

1. **Download Blender**
   - Go to [Blender.org](https://www.blender.org/) and download the **macOS version** suitable for your machine.

2. **Open the DMG File**
   - Find the downloaded `.dmg` file in your **Downloads** folder.
   - **Double-click** on the `.dmg` file to **mount** the disk image.

3. **Install Blender**
   - **Drag and drop** `Blender.app` to the **Applications** folder.

4. **First Launch of Blender**
   - Open **Finder** → **Applications** and double-click on `Blender.app` to launch.
   - If a security warning appears from macOS, proceed to: **System Preferences** → **Security & Privacy** → **Allow Blender to Run**.

Portable Installation (Optional)

So that all of the settings, add-ons, and configurations stay within the Blender folder, a **fully self-contained** version of Blender (so that when you install Blender, it should be installed like a **Portable Installation** and not installed like the normal, usual installation with-in the `Applications` folder), install a **Portable Installation** instead.

Updating Blender on macOS

Blender does **not** update automatically, so you'll need to install updates manually.

1. **Download the Latest Blender Version**
   - Visit [Blender.org](https://www.blender.org/) and download the newest `.dmg` file.

2. **Replace the Old Version**
   - Open Finder → **Applications and delete or replace** the existing `Blender.app`.
   - To keep a few versions, rename the old `Blender.app` (e.g., `Blender 4.1.app`).

3. **Running the New Blender Version**
   - Open **Finder** → **Applications** → **Blender.app**.

Additional Resources
   - **Importing Settings from Previous Versions:** The **Splash Screen Defaults** page provides information on moving settings when updating Blender.

Installing Blender on Windows

Before you proceed with installing Blender, visit the **Downloading Blender** page to check the **minimum system requirements** and download the appropriate version for your **Windows architecture.**

Important Note:

Blender supports both **x64 (64-bit)** and **ARM64** CPU architectures on Windows. Make sure to **download the appropriate version** that matches your **CPU architecture.**

Installation Methods

There are three methods of installing Blender:

1. Install from Windows Installer File (Recommended)
This is the easiest and most user-friendly installation method.

Steps:
1. **Download Blender**
   - Visit [Blender.org](https://www.blender.org/) and download the **Windows Installer.**

2. **Run the Installer**
   - **Double-click** the downloaded `.exe` file to start the installation.
   - Choose an **installation folder.**
   - Click **Install** and allow the process to complete.

3. **Complete the Installation**
   - The installer will:
   - ☑ Create an **entry in the Start Menu.**
   - ☑ **Configure `.blend` files** to open using Blender.

4. **Launch Blender**
   - Open **Start Menu** → **Blender** to run the program.

2. Install from ZIP File (Portable Installation)

If you prefer a **self-contained installation** that does not require administrator rights, use the **ZIP file method.**

Steps:
1. Download the ZIP File

- Visit [Blender.org](https://www.blender.org/) and download the **ZIP version** of Blender.

2. Extract the ZIP File

- Unpack the ZIP file with **Windows Explorer** or **WinRAR/7-Zip** into a directory of your preference (e.g., `C:\\\\Blender` or `D:\\\\Software\\\\Blender`).

3. Launch Blender

- In the extracted folder, **double-click** `blender.exe` to start it.

4. (Optional) Register Blender File Associations

- Since there isn't a ZIP version that accomplishes this for `.blend` files automatically, you can:
- Go to **Edit > Preferences > System**, then click **Register**.
- Alternatively, open Command Prompt and run: ``` blender -r ```

☑ Advantages of ZIP Installation:

- No **administrator rights** required.
- Can have **multiple versions** of Blender installed.

3. Install from Microsoft Store

If you want an **automatic installation and update process,** install Blender from the **Microsoft Store.**

Steps:
1. **Open the Microsoft Store**
   - Click **Start Menu** → Search for **Microsoft Store**.

2. **Search for Blender**
   - Type "Blender" in the search bar.
   - Click **Install** to download and install it.

3. **Launch Blender**
   - Open **Start Menu** → **Blender.**

✅ **Advantages of Microsoft Store Installation:**
   - **Automatic updates** when a new version is available.

Updating Blender on Windows

Since Blender does **not** have a built-in updater, you'll need to **manually update it.**

1. Updating using Windows Installer File (Recommended)
1. **Obtain the latest version** from [Blender.org](https://www.blender.org/).
2. **Run the new installer** and install in the same manner.
3. (**Optional) Uninstall the old one** via **Control Panel > Programs & Features.**

2. Updating using ZIP File
1. **Obtain the latest ZIP version** from [Blender.org](https://www.blender.org/).
2. **Copy it to a new folder** (e.g., `C:\\\\Blender_4.2`).

3. Run `blender.exe` from the new folder.

☑ **Tip**: You **don't need to uninstall the previous version**. You can have multiple versions of Blender installed.

 3. Updating from Microsoft Store
If you have installed Blender from the **Microsoft Store**, updates will be **automatically downloaded and installed.**

- **Importing Settings from Previous Versions:** The **Splash Screen Defaults** page provides the instructions for importing settings during the upgrade in Blender.

Installing Blender from Steam (Windows, macOS, Linux)

Steam is a popular software distribution platform that allows you to **download, install, and update Blender** seamlessly on **Windows, macOS, and Linux.**

How to Install Blender via Steam

1. **Download and Install Steam**
   - Visit [store.steampowered.com](https://store.steampowered.com/about/) and download the Steam client for your operating system.
   - Install Steam and **log in** or create a new account.

2. Search for Blender on Steam

- Open Steam and go to the **Store** tab.
- Type "**Blender**" in the search bar.
- Click on **Blender** from the search results.

3. Install Blender

- Click the **Install** button to begin downloading Blender.
- Once installed, Blender will be available in the **Library** tab of Steam.

☑ **Advantages of Installing via Steam:**

- **Automatic updates** whenever a new version is released.
- **Easier installation** and management for users already familiar with Steam.

Important Notes for Linux & Windows Users

- When installing Blender via Steam on **Windows or Linux,** **.blend files** will **not** automatically be associated with Blender.

To manually associate **.blend files**, follow the instructions in the **Windows** or **Linux installation guides:**

- **Windows**: Register `.blend` files in **Preferences > System** or run: ```blender -r```
- **Linux:** Create file associations in your **file manager settings.**

Updating Blender via Steam

One of the key benefits of using Steam is **automatic updates.**

- When a new version of Blender is released, **Steam will update it automatically** in the background.

- You don't need to manually download or install updates.

This makes Steam a great choice for users who want to keep Blender **always up to date** with minimal effort.

Linux Windowing Environment for Blender

Both **X11** and **Wayland** are supported by Blender on Linux. If Wayland is discovered, it will be **default-preferred**, otherwise **X11** will be used.

☑ How to Check Your Windowing Environment
- Open **Blender**
- Navigate to **Topbar** → **Blender** → **About Blender**

X11 Windowing System

X11 has been the most widely used **windowing environment** on Linux and Unix systems for decades.

Current Status: Still actively supported, with no plans for deprecation.

Advantages:
- **Stable & well-tested** across distributions
- **Good compatibility** with NVIDIA GPUs
- **Reliable window positioning**

Limitations:
- No smooth scrolling

- No native multi-touch gestures
- **Cursor warping issues** (cursor can leave the window when making rapid movements)

Wayland Windowing System

Wayland is a newer **Linux windowing environment** that offers more security and smoother performance.

Tested with:
- Gnome-Shell (Mutter)
- KDE (Plasma)
- SWAY (wlroots-based compositors)

Requirements (for users of GNOME):
- **libdecor** (found in the majority of Linux distributions)
- In case **libdecor** is not available, Blender will **use X11 as a fallback**

Advantages:
- ☑ Smooth trackpad scrolling
- ☑ Support for multi-touch gestures
- ☑ Robust cursor warping

Limitations:
- ✖ **No support for window positioning** (affects drag-and-drop between windows)
- ✖ **NVIDIA GPUs may experience flickering, glitches, or crashes** due to not completely supported drivers

- ✖ **Older versions of GNOME (prior to GNOME 44) have fractional scaling** issues

Resolving Wayland Issues in Blender

Explore Wayland Logs
For debugging issues, launch **debugging enabled** Blender:

The publication of this page does not imply endorsement of the content.

1 **Blender's Internal Wayland Logs** ```` ```sh blender --log "ghost.wl." --log-level 2``` ````

2 **Wayland Built-In Logging** ```` ```sh WAYLAND_DEBUG=1 blender``` ````

Force X11 Instead of Wayland

If you're experiencing trouble on Wayland, you can **force Blender to use X11:** ```` ```sh WAYLAND_DISPLAY="" blender``` ````

✅ **For NVIDIA Users:** As Wayland support in NVIDIA drivers is partial, a transition to X11 is usually the best option.

Disable Window Borders on GNOME (Wayland)

Blender utilizes **libdecor** as a window decorator in GNOME. If you require a **borderless window**, you can simply disable it: ```sh DISPLAY=" " blender```

You can also **uninstall libdecor** and get the same result.

Environment Variables for Cursor Settings

When you need to modify **cursor size or theme** on Wayland:

- **Set a custom cursor theme** ```sh export XCURSOR_THEME="your_theme_name"```

- **Scale cursor size (default is 28)** ```sh export XCURSOR_SIZE=36```
(Good for Hi-DPI screens)

Feature Comparison: X11 vs. Wayland

Feature	X11	Wayland
Smooth scrolling (trackpad)	✖	☑
Multi-touch gestures (pinch-to-zoom, pan, orbit)	✖	☑

Strong cursor warping (for object transformation)	✖	☑
Window positioning support (restore, dragging)	☑	✖

>

>\ X11 cursor warping has the ability to cause the cursor to escape the window when moving it rapidly.

Which One Should You Use?

☑ If you **appreciate stability and compatibility, X11** is your best option, especially for **NVIDIA users.**

☑ If you **want smoother performance and touch gestures**, **Wayland** is the preferable option (on AMD & Intel GPUs).

Chapter 3

Blender's Initial Setup and Customization

First-Time Preferences

When you start out with Blender, you might be interested in **setting some of the preferences** to suit your needs. These are some major preferences that you may wish to set.

Setting Interface Language

It is possible for Blender to operate in more than one language. To activate the translation:

1. Go **Edit → Preferences → Interface**
2. Select the option for **Translation**
3. Choose your preferred **Language**
4. Select what you want to translate (**Interface, Tooltips, New Data)**

For more details, refer to **Language Settings.**

Setting Input Preferences

Keyboard Shortcuts

If your keyboard does not support a separate number pad, enable:

☑ **Edit → Preferences → Input → Keyboard → Emulate Numpad**
This allows you to use the **regular number keys** instead of a numpad for 3D navigation.

Mouse Controls

If your mouse **does not have a middle button,** turn on:

☑ **Edit → Preferences → Input → Mouse → Emulate 3 Button Mouse**
This allows you to **hold Alt (or OSKey)** while dragging to orbit the 3D view.

For further customization, see **Input Preferences.**

File and Paths Configuration

Set default applications for file handling under:

☑ **Edit → Preferences → File Paths**

You can specify:
- **Default Image Editor** (e.g., GIMP, Krita)
- **Animation Player** for playback
- **Temporary Directory** for auto-saves and temporary renders

Tip: Paths with `//` at the beginning are **relative to the where the current blend file is.**

For further options, please see **File Preferences.**

Save & Load Settings

⚠ Auto Run Python Scripts

If you spend a lot of time working on **complicated rigs and automations**, it may be beneficial to have Python scripts auto-run.

☑ **Edit → Preferences → Save & Load → Auto Run Python Scripts**

⚠ **Note:** This option protects against **malicious scripts** in downloaded blend files. Enable it **only if you trust the source** of your files.

These early settings help **streamline your workflow** and **give a smoother experience** in Blender.

Peripheral Configuration for Blender

In order to have the best experience with Blender, it is important to **correctly configure your peripherals.** They include your **display, keyboard, mouse, graphic tablet, and 3D mouse (NDOF device).**

1 Display Configuration

- A **Full HD (1920x1080) display** or higher is recommended.
- **Multi-monitor setups** are also supported, with workspaces spanning across screens.

Tip: Arrange your monitors in your operating system's display settings for a more efficient workflow.

2 Input Devices

Keyboard
- A **keyboard with a numeric keypad** is preferable.

- **English (UK/US) layouts** are ideal for Blender's default keymap.

Tip: If you are using a non-English keyboard, attempt switching to the **UK or US layout** when working within Blender.

Mouse
- A **3-button mouse with a scroll wheel** is ideal.
- If your mouse **does not have a middle button**, enable **Mouse Button Emulation** at:

☑ **Edit → Preferences → Input → Mouse → Emulate 3 Button Mouse**

How it works:

Mouse Type	Left Click (LMB)	Middle Click (MMB)	Right Click (RMB)
3-Button Mouse	LMB	MMB	RMB
2-Button Mouse	**LMB**	**Alt + LMB**	RMB

Numpad Emulation (For Keyboards Without a Numpad)

If your keyboard **does not have a numeric keypad,** enable:

- ☑ **Edit → Preferences → Input → Keyboard → Emulate Numpad**
- Enables the use of the **top number row** for Blender shortcuts, but **you will lose the original functions** (e.g., switching between vertex/edge/face selection in Edit Mode).

Tip: Consider using an **external numpad** for a more comfortable workflow.

Graphic Tablet

- Blender supports **graphic tablets** for sculpting and texture painting.
- **Pressure sensitivity** and other stylus features work **out-of-the-box**.

NDOF (3D Mouse) Device

- These devices allow for **precise 3D navigation.**
- Works well for professionals using Blender for **modeling, CAD, or animation**.

Properly setting up your **input and display devices optimizes** your Blender experience. **Do you need assistance with setting up your key bindings or shortcuts?**

Setting up Head-Mounted Displays (HMDs) in Blender

Virtual Reality support in Blender makes it possible to **engage in immersive 3D environments** through HMDs (Head-Mounted

Displays). The hardware **traces head positions** and provides virtual environments in small screens that are placed directly in front of the user's eyes, and the user would feel as though they are actually inside the environment.

Blender's VR support is based on the **OpenXR standard**, which is **multi-platform** and, therefore, under development and prone to varied levels of support on different devices.

Supported VR Platforms

Blender currently supports a variety of VR platforms with the aid of OpenXR. An overview of the supported devices and their compatibility can be seen in the following:

Platform	Operating System	Notes
HTC Vive Cosmos	Windows	Developer Preview
HTC Vive Focus 3	Windows	Developer Preview
Monado (Open Source XR for Linux)	GNU/Linux	Not yet suggested for use by the general public
Meta (Oculus Rift & Quest)	Windows	Oculus v31 Update necessary; Oculus Link necessary for Quest

SteamVR	Windows, GNU/Linux	Must be on SteamVR 1.16 or newer
Varjo	Windows	Supported in full
Windows Mixed Reality	Windows	Must be installed alongside Windows 10 May 2019 Update (1903)

Configuring Your HMD in Blender

To use VR within Blender, you must **set up your HMD and enable the VR Scene Inspection add-on.**

HTC Vive Cosmos & HTC Vive Focus 3
Those headsets are **in Developer Preview**, and therefore can **lack full features.**

Setup Steps:
1. Finish the setup from the **Vive Developer Forums.**
2. In Blender, enable: **Edit → Preferences → Add-ons → VR Scene Inspection.**

Monado (Linux Open Source XR Platform)

- **Monado** is an open-source VR platform for **Linux**, but it's **not yet ready for full production use.**
- Supported on **Ubuntu (Eoan, Focal)** and **Debian (bullseye, sid).**

Setup Steps:
1. Install Monado from the **official Getting Started Guide.**
2. In Blender, turn on: **Edit → Preferences → Add-ons → VR Scene Inspection.**

Meta (Oculus Rift & Quest)

Meta's VR headsets **completely support OpenXR** since the **Oculus v31 update.**

Setup Steps:
1. **Download & Install** Oculus Rift/Oculus Link software.
2. Open the **Oculus App → General Tab →** Set **Oculus as the active OpenXR runtime.**

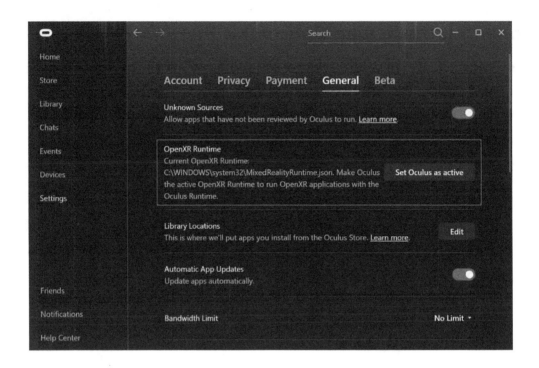

3. Turn on in Blender: **Edit → Preferences → Add-ons → VR Scene Inspection**

Passthrough Support:
- Passthrough (seeing your real world when in VR) is **turned off** by default for Oculus Link.
- Turn it on manually in the **Quest Link App settings.**

For best performance, use **a direct USB connection** or **Ethernet connection on your computer.**

SteamVR (HTC Vive, Oculus, Windows Mixed Reality)

SteamVR **fully supports OpenXR** starting from **SteamVR 1.16.**

Setup Steps:
1. Open **SteamVR → Developer Tab → Set SteamVR as the active OpenXR runtime**.
2. In Blender, enable: **Edit → Preferences → Add-ons → VR Scene Inspection**.

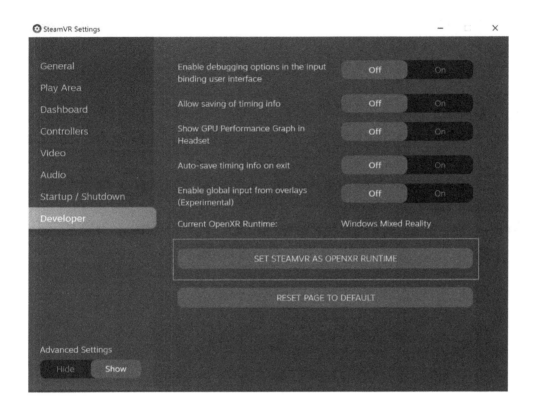

Tip: SteamVR can also be used for HTC Vive Cosmos, Oculus, and Windows Mixed Reality headsets.

Varjo
Varjo headsets **fully support OpenXR.**

Setup Steps:
1. **Install Varjo Base Software.**

2. In Blender, enable: **Edit → Preferences → Add-ons → VR Scene Inspection**.

Windows Mixed Reality (WMR)

Windows Mixed Reality supports OpenXR **on Windows 10 (May 2019 Update or later).**

Setup Steps:
1. **Verify compatibility** with the **Windows Mixed Reality PC Check** tool.
2. **Open the Mixed Reality Portal →** Click **"." (Menu Button) →** Select **"Set Up OpenXR".**
3. In Blender, enable: **Edit → Preferences → Add-ons → VR Scene Inspection**.

Switching OpenXR Runtimes:

If you have already used **SteamVR** or **Oculus**, switch back to WMR by:

☑ Installing **OpenXR Developer Tools** from the **Microsoft Store.**
☑ Turning on **Windows Mixed Reality as the active runtime.**

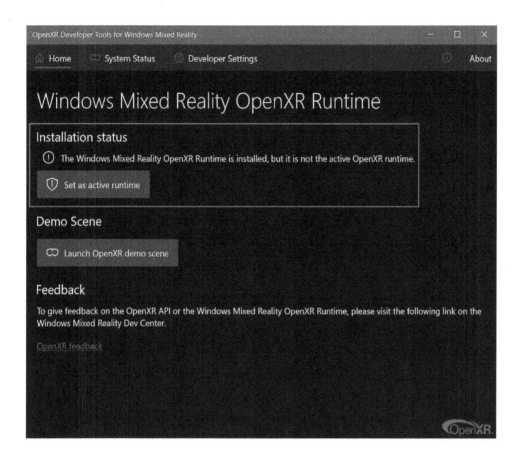

Blender's VR support is **constantly improving,** but full functionality depends on your **HMD, operating system, and OpenXR support.** Once installed, you can **render 3D scenes in VR**, enabling modeling, sculpting, and designing for immersive space.

Blender Defaults & Initial Preferences

The first time you start **Blender** or after an update, you'll be prompted to create a few **initial settings** via the **Splash Screen.** These are the preferences which determine **how you will interact with Blender** and can later be changed via the **Preferences menu.**

Importing Preferences from a Previous Version

If you've ever used a **past version of Blender**, you can **import preferences** instead of having to manually re-tweak everything.

What is imported?
- ✅ **User Preferences** (theme, keymap, language, etc.)
- ✅ **Startup Files** (default scene and UI settings)

Why import preferences?
Each version of Blender **maintains its configuration files separate**, so importing gives you a **seamless transition** between versions.

Creating New Preferences

If you prefer **a fresh start,** you can set up new preferences manually.

Language
Choose the **interface language.**
More customization options are available under **Translation Preferences.**

Theme
Select between **Light** and **Dark** mode.
Other color customizations can be done in **Preferences → Themes.**

Keymap (Keyboard Shortcuts)

Choose the **default keyboard shortcut configuration:**

- **Blender (Default)** – The standard keymap of Blender.
- **Blender 2.7x** – For users who are migrating from earlier versions of Blender.
- **Industry Compatible** – Mimics keymaps from other 3D software like Maya or 3ds Max.

Learn more about Blender keymaps **here**.

Mouse Select
Select if **Right-Click** or **Left-Click** should be used for selecting.

Spacebar Action
Defines the action taken on pressing the **Spacebar**:

- **Play** → Plays animation back (best suited for animators & video editors).
- **Tools** → Toggles on the Toolbar at the current cursor location (best suited for modeling & rigging).
- **Search** → Opens a searchable menu (best for beginners).

Saving & Managing Preferences

Saving Preferences
✅ Blender **automatically saves preferences** when changed.
✅ To manually save a new startup file:
  File → Defaults → Save Startup File.

Where Blender Stores Defaults
Blender has **two main default files:**

1. **Preferences File** – Saves **themes, keymaps, and add-ons.**
2. **Startup File** – Saves **default scenes and UI layouts.**

Resetting Blender to Factory Defaults

If you wish to **return Blender to default settings**, do the following:

- **Reset Preferences Only** → **Preferences** → **Load Factory Settings.**
- **Reset Both Preferences & Startup File** → **File** → **Defaults** → **Load Factory Settings.**

Note: When factory settings are loaded, preferences **won't auto-save** again unless saved again manually.

Blender gives you a **tweakable setup** for **new users, migrating users, and pros.** Irrespective of whether you **import settings** or **start from scratch**, you can afterward tweak anything in **Preferences**.

Blender Help System

Blender offers a number of built-in and web-based help features to help users make sense of its interface and tools.

1 Tooltips: Quick On-Screen Help

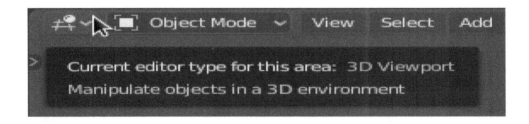

Blender includes **tooltips**, which pop up if you hover the mouse over a button or option for a second or two.

Elements in a Tooltip

A tooltip can include the following:

✔️ **Short Description** – Brief description of the tool or environment.

✔️ **Shortcut** – Keyboard or mouse shortcut for quick access.

✔️ **Value** – Displays the current value of a property.

✔️ **Color Swatch** – An enlarged preview is displayed by hovering over a color property, as well as **Hex, RGBA, and HSVA** values.

✔️ **Library** – Indicates the source file in case the object is referenced in another project.

✔️ **Disabled (Red Text)** – Explains why a property is **not editable.**

✔️ **Python Code** – When Python Tooltips are enabled, the corresponding Python expression for scripting is displayed.

Context-Sensitive Manual Access

If you need help with a tool or setting, Blender has the facility to **access relevant documentation directly** inside the software.

Getting to the Manual for a Tool

Hover over the tool or setting.

- **Press F1** or right-click and select **Online Manual** from the context menu.
- Blender will open the **official documentation** of the provided tool in a web browser.

Note: Not all tools have a direct link to documentation. If unavailable, Blender can display an **info header alert** or lead you to a **general section** of the manual.

Help Menu: Web Resources & Support

The **Help Menu** (top bar) provides direct links to **Blender-related resources,** including:

✓ **Official Blender Manual** – Complete documentation for Blender.

✓ **Release Notes** – Highlights changes and enhancements in the new version of Blender.

✓ **Tutorials** – Access multiple **official and community** tutorials.

✓ **Support** – Direct links to professional and community support.

✓ **User Communities** – Access to Blender user forums and communities.

✓ **Report a Bug** – Direct link to **Blender's Bug Tracker** (Registration is necessary).

Saving System Information

Saving system information by Blender is possible for debugging issues.

How to Save System Info:
- Go to **Help** → **Save System Info**
Save the generated **system-info.txt** file.

What does System Info contain?

✅ **Blender Version & Build Information** – Version, type of build, and installation path.

✅ **Python Settings** – Path and version installed of Python.

✅ **Directories** – Paths to script directories, paths to data files directories, preset directory paths, and paths to temp file directories (in Preferences).

✅ **GPU Info** – Driver version, name of vendor, and supported capabilities.

✅ **Enabled Add-Ons** – Shows all enabled add-ons.

This information proves useful when **debugging errors, reporting bugs**, or **tuning performance.**

Blender's **help system** is designed to be **fast, informative, and interactive**. Either via **tooltips, built-in documentation access**, or **online resources,** you'll always receive the assistance when you need it.

PART TWO:

WORKING WITH BLENDER'S USER INTERFACE

Blender's user interface (UI) is a highly capable and versatile system that can support a vast array of creative work processes. Whether modeling, animating, sculpting, or rendering, Blender offers an accessible yet incredibly flexible interface that can help streamline productivity.

This part of the guide will walk you through the central components of Blender's UI, walking you through navigating, initializing, and fine-tuning your workspace for an optimal experience. By the end of this section, you should have a good understanding of how Blender's interface works and how to tailor it to your needs.

Topics Covered in This Section:

1. Window System
Blender's window system is built on a unique windowing system that is highly customizable. This chapter covers how windows, regions, and areas cooperate to give a smooth working environment.

- **Introduction**: Overview of Blender's window system.
- **Splash Screen**: What the first screen looks like when starting Blender.
- **Topbar**: The top toolbar for scene and workflow control.

- **Workspaces**: Integrated configurations of the various tasks such as modeling, animation, and rendering.
- **Status Bar**: Displays critical information like memory usage, statistics, and notifications.

2. Areas and Regions

Blender divides its interface into areas and regions. In this chapter, how they are implemented and how you can configure them is described.

- **Areas**: Major components of the interface that comprise multiple editors.
- **Regions**: Sub-units within areas that include toolbars and panels.
- **Tabs & Panels:** Units for organization that segregate tools and settings.

3. Keymap and Shortcuts

Blender highly relies on shortcuts, and as such, key mappings must be known to perform effectively.

- **Common Shortcuts:** Regular keyboard and mouse shortcuts.
- **Default Keymap**: Blender's default shortcut arrangement.
- **Industry-Compatible Keymap**: Yet another keymap, one suitable for professionals well-versed with other 3D tools like Maya and 3ds Max.

4. UI Elements and Controls

Blender's UI is made up of several interactive components. Knowledge about these elements will make navigation and workflow easier.

- **Buttons:** Action initiators used to invoke commands.
- **Input Fields:** Numerical or text values that can be adjusted.
- **Menus:** Drop-down menus that group functions and tools.
- **Eyedropper:** A device for picking colors or choosing scene items.
- **Decorators:** Status indicators for user changes and auto-saving.
- **Data-Block Menu:** A mechanism for handling associated data.
- **List View:** Shows groups of elements like materials, objects, and layers.

5. Color and Curve Widgets

Blender possesses various tools for managing color and curves, which are applied in shading, compositing, and animation.

- **Color Picker:** Color picking and editing.
- **Color Ramp Widget:** Color management via gradients.
- **Color Palette:** Saving and reusing color schemes.
- **Curve Widget:** Animation and shader property editing via curves.

6. Tools and Operators

Blender has an interactive tool system and operators for performing various editing operations.

- **Tool System:** A brief overview of Blender's interactive tools.
- **Operators:** Operators used for object and scene editing.
- **Undo & Redo:** Undoing changes and revisions.
- **Annotations:** Adding comments and sketches in Blender.

7. Selecting and Manipulating Objects

Selection is a fundamental skill in Blender. This chapter covers different selection techniques and how to manipulate objects.

- **Selecting**: Choosing objects, vertices, edges, and faces.
  - **Nodes:** Working with Blender's node-based system.
  - **Node Parts:** Components of a node.
  - **Arranging Nodes:** Organizing node setups for better workflow.
  - **Editing Nodes:** Adjusting and customizing node properties.
  - **Sidebar & Node Groups:** Performance organizing of node collections.
  - **Frame & Reroute Nodes:** Readability organizing of complex node trees.

This section of the guide will give you the background information to be comfortable with Blender's interface. Each chapter will break down these UI elements in fine detail, and provide you with the skills you'll need to optimize your workflow and improve your overall Blender experience.

And now, **Chapter 4: Window System,** in which we will observe how Blender's interface is structured and how you can make it fit your workflow.

CHAPTER 4:

USING THE WINDOW SYSTEM IN BLENDER 2025

Here we discuss how the Blender interface is structured and how you can customize it to suit your requirements to improve your workflow. Blender's interface is designed to be highly flexible so that users can structure and personalize their workspace in ways that accommodate different tasks. Unlike traditional software with static window arrangements, Blender employs a modular **window system,** in which areas, known as **Areas,** can be resized, split, or merged as desired.

This chapter provides you with a comprehensive knowledge of Blender's window system so that you can navigate and set up your workspace efficiently to achieve maximum productivity.

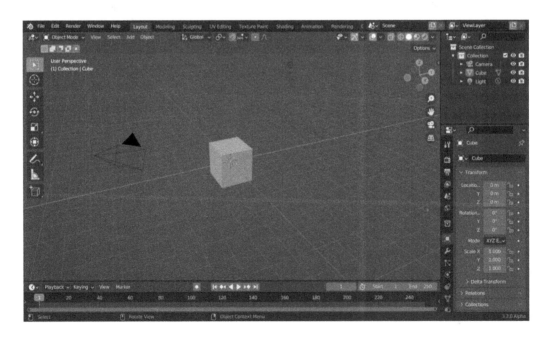

The Blender's Window System

Blender's **window system** is designed for flexibility and efficiency, allowing users to arrange, split, merge, and customize their interface to fit their specific workflow. Unlike traditional software, where windows and panels have fixed layouts, Blender employs a **modular system** that lets you create a workspace tailored to your needs.

This modularity is crucial because Blender is an **all-in-one** tool for various tasks, including **modeling, sculpting, animation, rendering, compositing, and video editing.** Each of these tasks requires a different workspace setup, and Blender's window system makes it easy to switch between them seamlessly.

Understanding Blender's Window System Structure

Blender's interface is structured using a **hierarchical system** of **Windows, Areas, and Regions.** Here's a breakdown of how it works:

1. Blender Window
The entire Blender interface is contained within a **single window,** called the **Blender Window.** This window holds all the different panels and workspaces you interact with.

You can have multiple Blender windows open at the same time, especially when working with multiple monitors.

2. Areas

Within the Blender window, the interface is divided into multiple **Areas**. An Area is a section of the interface that serves a specific function. Examples include:

- **3D Viewport:** The main workspace where you interact with your 3D scene.
- **Shader Editor:** A node-based editor for creating materials and shaders.
- **Timeline:** Used for animation playback and keyframe management.
- **Outliner:** Displays a hierarchical list of all objects in your scene.

Each **Area** can be resized, split, or merged, allowing you to **rearrange the layout** as needed.

3. Regions

Inside each **Area**, you'll find **Regions**, which contain menus, toolbars, and settings. These Regions help you interact with Blender's tools and features.

For example, in the **3D Viewport,** the **Tool Shelf (T)** and **Properties Region (N)** are part of the Regions within that Area.

Why is Blender's Window System Important?

1. Customization & Efficiency

Blender's window system allows you to create an **optimized workspace.** For example, if you're sculpting, you might want a large 3D Viewport with the Sculpting Tools on the side. If you're animating, you may prefer to have the **Graph Editor** and **Dope Sheet** visible alongside the 3D Viewport.

2. Multi-Monitor Support

If you have multiple screens, you can **open extra Blender windows** and arrange them across monitors. This is useful when working on complex projects where you need multiple views at once.

3. Seamless Navigation Between Workspaces
Blender's modular system allows you to **quickly switch** between different workspace layouts (e.g., Modeling, Sculpting, Animation, etc.), making it easy to adapt to different tasks.

Key Features of Blender's Window System

1. **Non-Overlapping UI** – Unlike many 3D applications that use floating panels, Blender's interface is clean and free from overlapping windows, making it easier to focus on your work.
2. **Split and Merge Areas** – You can divide any Area into two smaller sections or merge two Areas together, creating a **fully customized** layout.
3. **Workspaces for Specific Tasks** – Blender provides **pre-configured workspaces** for different workflows, such as Modeling, Sculpting, Animation, and Video Editing.
4. **Multi-Window Support** – Open additional Blender windows on different monitors for a **more expansive workspace.**
5. **Persistent Layouts** – Blender remembers your **custom UI arrangement,** so when you reopen your project, your layout remains unchanged.

How to Navigate Blender's Window System

To **move through Blender's interface smoothly**, you need to understand the following:

1. **Resizing Areas**
   - Hover over the **border** between two Areas until the **resize cursor** appears.
   - **Click and drag** to resize the Area.

2. **Splitting an Area**
   - Move your cursor to the **top-right or bottom-left corner** of an Area until a **crosshair cursor** appears.
   - **Click and drag** to split the Area into two sections.

3. **Merging Areas**
   - Right-click on the **border** between two Areas.
   - Choose **"Join Areas"** and select the direction of the merge.

4. **Switching Workspaces**
   - Use the **Workspace Tabs** at the top of the interface.
   - Press **Ctrl + Page Up/Page Down** to cycle through workspaces.

5. **Opening a New Blender Window**
   - Go to **Window → New Window** to open a separate Blender window.

Blender's window system is **one of its most powerful features**, allowing you to **customize your workspace** for maximum efficiency. Whether you're working on a **single monitor** or a **multi-screen setup,** Blender gives you **full control** over your layout.

In the next section, we'll take a **closer look at the Splash Screen**, which appears when you first open Blender and gives you quick access to recent files, settings, and new projects.

CHAPTER 5

NAVIGATING THE SPLASH SCREEN AND TOPBAR IN BLENDER

When you first launch Blender, the **Splash Screen** is the one that you will first see. The screen is a **quick-access platform,** and from there, you can **launch recently opened projects, adjust preferences, and apply settings** prior to actually beginning your work. While it may be perceived as a trivial feature, the Splash Screen assists in greatly **streamlining your workflow** and preparing Blender to the manner in which you need it to be prepared.

Understanding the Splash Screen

The Splash Screen is divided into several key sections:

1. **Blender Version & Logo** – Displays the current Blender version and branding.
2. **New File Templates** – Allows you to start a project using predefined settings for different workflows.
3. **Recent Files** – A quick way to open recently worked-on projects.
4. **General Options & Preferences** – Provides you with shortcuts to importing settings, accessing manuals, and initial setup of Blender.
5. **Dismiss Button** – Click anywhere on the Splash Screen outside of it to dismiss it and start working in Blender.

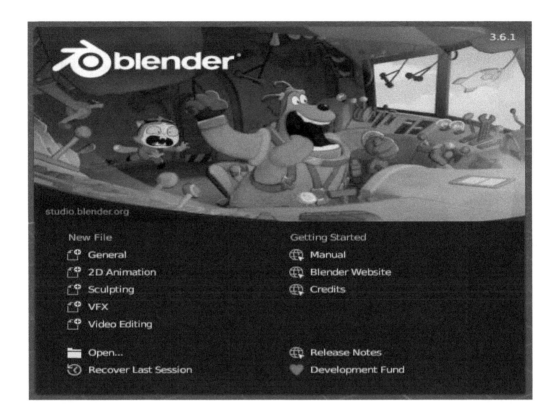

All of these types are **created so that you can start right away**, whether you're opening up an old file, getting ready to set up a new one, or modifying preferences in advance.

Splash Screen Important Features

1. Blender Version & Logo

Top of the Splash Screen is where the **Blender version number** and the Blender logo appear. This comes in handy as Blender is continuously being updated, and it informs you of what version you have. If you are on a **collaborative project,** it can be worth checking to see if they will be compatible.

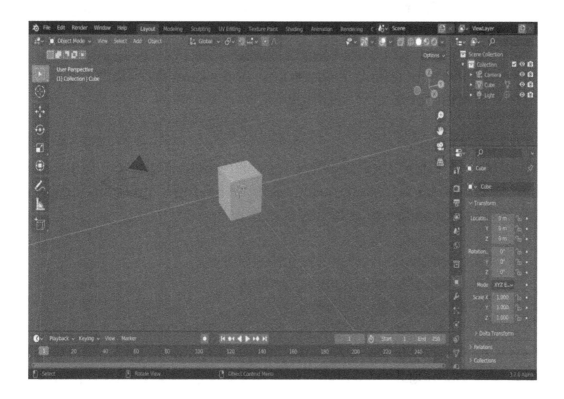

2. New File Templates

One of the best features of the Splash Screen is that you can **launch a new project with different configurations**. Instead of having to manually configure every aspect of your scene, you can choose a **pre-defined template** which will be optimal for you according to your work. The templates are:

- **General** – A standard layout with standard settings for modeling, animation, and rendering.
- **2D Animation** – A special place for 2D animation using Grease Pencil.
- **Sculpting** – Pre-made settings for digital sculpting.
- **VFX** – A place intended for visual effects and compositing.

- **Video Editing** – A special place for video editing and sequencing.

Choosing the right template saves time and allows **Blender to launch with the right tools and settings** for your workflow.

3. Recent Files
The **Recent Files** area displays recently opened projects, and you can easily get back to work quickly without having to navigate through file folders. This feature is handy for:

- Fast access to work-in-progress projects
- Avoiding manually hunting for files
- Preserving session continuity

Every entry shows the **file name, save directory, and thumbnail preview,** allowing it to be identified more easily as the correct project.

4. General Options & Preferences

Below the Recent Files, you have **more options** for setting up Blender prior to beginning your work. They include:

a) Import Preferences from Previous Version
If you have upgraded to a newer version of Blender, you don't have to redo all your settings manually. Choosing this option **imports preferences automatically,** including:
- **Keymaps** (keyboard shortcuts)
- **Themes** (color scheme and layout of the interface)
- **Add-ons** (installed extensions)
- **Startup files**

This ensures that you have a **consistent workflow** even when you upgrade to a newer version of Blender.

b) Create New Preferences

You can choose this option if you wish to have a **fresh start** with the new version. It will set Blender to **default settings,** as long as clean. You can use it if you prefer to **test new features without legacy settings interfering.**

c) Language & Theme Settings
- **Language** – You have the option of altering Blender's **user interface language,** specifically helpful for users who are not English speakers.
- **Theme** – Choose a **Light or Dark** UI theme. Additional customization possibilities are available within the **Preferences menu.**

d) Keymap Selection

The Keymap region enables you to choose among multiple sets of **keyboard shortcuts,** including:
- **Blender Default** – The standard shortcut configuration.
- **Blender 2.7x** – For users transitioning from earlier versions of Blender.
- **Industry Compatible** – For those who are already familiar with other 3D applications like Maya or 3ds Max.

Having the correct keymap loaded makes it easier to navigate, especially if you are transitioning from another 3D application.

e) Mouse Select

Blender allows you to choose whether to select objects using the **Left Mouse Button (LMB) or Right Mouse Button (RMB).**

- **Left Click Select** – This should be used by most users, since it is the norm to most programs.
- **Right Click Select** – Blender's traditional method, best for experienced users.

f) Spacebar Action
The **Spacebar key** has different functions based on your choice:
- **Play** – Starts playing animation.
- **Tools** – Opens Toolbar for convenient tool selection.
- **Search** – Opens search menu, which is convenient for new users.

This customization allows you to manage **Spacebar behavior** according to your workflow.

5. Dismissing the Splash Screen
Once you've made your choice, you can **dismiss the Splash Screen** by clicking outside of it or pressing **Esc**. This drops you right into Blender's world.

Why is the Splash Screen Important?

The Splash Screen **is not just a welcome screen**—it is a **productivity tool** which can:

☑ **Save time** by giving you instant access to recent documents.
☑ **Improve productivity in your workflow** using pre-defined templates.
☑ **Ensure a smooth transition** from Blender versions.
☑ **Make your experience your own** with choice of language, theme, and keymap.

For beginners, the **Splash Screen is an easy introduction,** and for power users, it provides its **shortcuts that save time and the degree of customization.**

The Splash Screen is a hugely beneficial feature which often goes ignored. By taking a few moments to learn about it, you can **streamline your workflow, get your work done more quickly,** and **set up Blender precisely as you prefer**.

The Blender Topbar

The **Blender Topbar** is a critical part of the user interface, serving as a command centre for **global options, workspace navigation, and tool settings.** It provides quick access to common functions and therefore is a significant feature towards improving workflow performance.

In contrast to certain interface components that vary based on context, the **Topbar is consistent** across workspaces, providing an uninterrupted experience in switching between activities such as **modeling, sculpting, animation, and rendering**.

Understanding the Topbar Layout

The **Topbar** spans along the top of the Blender interface and is comprised of **three principal sections:**

1. **Application Menu** – Has elementary file operations such as **New, Open, Save, Import, and Export.**
2. **Tool Settings** – Displays settings specific to the active tool, enabling instant customization.
3. **Workspaces Navigation** – Allows you to move between workspaces customized for specific use.

Every one of these sections is very important in the process of optimizing your workflow, with the view of having essential tools and settings handy at all times.

1. Application Menu

The **Application Menu** can be found at the top-left corner of the screen and contains access to core functions of a file-management nature and for the operation of the system as a whole. The following can be found under it:

a) File Menu
- **New** – Initializes a new Blender project.
- **Open.** – Opens an existing Blender project (.blend file).
- **Save / Save As.** – Saves the current project, leaving space for versioning.
- **Import / Export** – Exports in a variety of file formats, including **OBJ, FBX, STL, and GLTF.**
- **Append / Link** – Enables you to import objects, materials, or other content from another file within Blender.

The **File Menu** is crucial to keeping your projects well organized and your work in order and saved.

b) Edit Menu

The **Edit menu** provides access to:
- **Undo/Redo** – Allows you to undo or redo previous actions.
- **Preferences** – Opens the Blender Preferences window, where you can modify UI settings, keymaps, and add-ons.
- **Adjust Last Operation** – Shows parameters for last action, which can be easily changed.

c) Render Menu

This menu has options for **rendering images and animations.** You can:
- Render an image (F12) or animation (Ctrl + F12).
- See the rendered results in the Image Editor.
- Access Render Settings for tuning output quality.

d) Window Menu

This menu allows you to manage Blender's interface windows, including:
- Toggling full-screen mode.
- Opening a new Blender window.
- Displaying system information for debugging purposes.

e) Help Menu

Provides links to:
- The official Blender Manual.
- Tutorials for learning Blender.
- Bug reporting tools.

This page is particularly useful for new users who are looking for advice or experienced users who need to troubleshoot.

2. Tool Settings

The **Tool Settings section** in the Topbar gets dynamically updated based on the selected tool. This allows for quick **adjustment of brush settings, transformation properties, and other tool-specific options.**

For example:
- When using the **Move Tool,** options appear for **constraint axes and snapping settings.**
- In **Sculpt Mode**, you'll see settings for **brush size, strength, and stroke type.**
- In **Grease Pencil Mode,** it offers options for **stroke thickness, opacity, and blending modes.**

Why is the Tool Settings Section Important?

☑ **Quick access** to relevant tool settings.
☑ Reduces the need to open more panels.
☑ **Increases efficiency** with controls in one place.

3. Workspaces Navigation

Blender's interface is divided into **Workspaces**, each designed for a particular purpose. The **Workspaces Navigation section** in the Topbar allows you to **quickly switch between these workspaces.**

Default Workspaces

- **Layout** – General workspace for modeling, animation, and shading.
- **Modeling** – Contains tools optimal for creating and modifying 3D models.
- **Sculpting** – Packed with brushes and tools specialized for digital sculpting.
- **UV Editing** – Used for unwrapping and modifying UV maps used for texturing.
- **Texture Paint** – Provides the tools to paint directly on 3D objects.
- **Shading** – A space dedicated to the creation of material and shaders.
- **Animation** – Designed to animate objects, characters, and rigs.
- **Rendering** – Holds the settings for rendering and final output of high-quality images.
- **Compositing** – Applied to composite rendered images post-processing.
- **Scripting** – An environment to code Python scripts and automate procedures.

Custom Workspaces

Blender allows the creation and personalization of one's own workspace by rearranging the layout according to specific needs. This is more useful for a professional who demands a customized flow.

Workspaces Switching

- Open a **workspace tab** within the Topbar.
- To switch workspaces, use the shortcut **Ctrl + Page Up/Page Down.**
- Click the right-click on a tab to **rename, delete, or duplicate a workspace.**

Why is Workspaces Navigation Important?

☑ **Facilitates easy switching between tasks** without the UI being rearranged.

☑ Provides a smooth workflow for different sides of 3D production.

☑ Avoids distraction by displaying only the necessary tools for each task.

The Topbar is **a crucial aspect of Blender's interface**, giving you:

☑ **Good File Management** – Quick access to saving, opening, and exporting a project.

☑ **Dynamic Tool Adjusting** – Puts relevant settings in easy reach all the time.

☑ **Smooth Task Changing** – Moving between tasks is smooth and effortless.

Learning the **Topbar** will **significantly enhance your workflow,** allowing you to devote more time to thinking creatively and less time obstructing the interface.

The **Topbar** is one of the **most important and most utilized UI elements in Blender.** It provides you with a single location for **file operations, tool settings, and workspace management**, and therefore is essential for an optimal workflow.

In the next section, we'll explore **Workspaces in depth,** discussing how to customize, organize, and optimize them for different tasks.

Blender Workspaces

Blender workspaces are **pre-configured layouts** designed to streamline specific tasks such as **modeling, sculpting, shading, animation, rendering, and compositing.** Every workspace is designed with **panels, tools, and settings** unique to its function, reducing the need for manual adjustments and streamlining workflows.

Being aware of and effectively utilizing Workspaces can **save time, keep things in better order, and lead to greater productivity** by displaying only the necessary tools to execute a particular task.

Learning Blender's Workspace System

Blender possesses a **action-based UI design,** where each workspace is meant to be utilized for a specific action. The **Workspaces Navigation bar,** which is displayed in the **Topbar,** makes it easy to transition between workspaces.

Every workspace includes:

☑ **Various editors** laid out to cater to the task in mind.

☑ **Personalized tools and menus** specific to the chosen workspace.

☑ **Resizable layouts** that can be configured to a user's liking.

Users can navigate through workspaces by using:
- The **top-level workspace tabs.**
- The shortcut **Ctrl + Page Up / Page Down.**

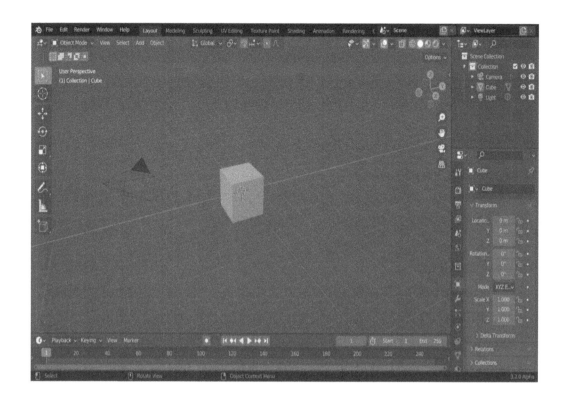

Default Workspaces in Blender

Blender has a number of **default workspaces**, each tailored for a specific part of 3D production. Let's dive into them:

1. Layout Workspace

The **Layout** workspace is the **default startup** when Blender is launched. It is intended for general use, such as **viewing, selecting, transforming, and handling objects.**

Key Features:

☑ **3D Viewport** to work with objects.

☑ **Outliner** to work with scene hierarchy.

☑ **Properties Editor** to handle object properties and settings.

☑ **Timeline** to have basic control of animation.

This workspace is well-suited to prepare a scene prior to venturing into dedicated workflows such as modeling or animation.

2. Modeling Workspace

The **Modeling** workspace provides tools and settings specifically tailored for creating and editing 3D geometry.

Major Features:

☑ **3D Viewport** with a dedicated toolbar for modeling operations.

☑ **Modifiers Panel** for non-destructive modeling techniques.

☑ **Mesh Editing Tools** like Extrude, Bevel, Knife, and Loop Cut.

☑ **Wireframe and Solid Shading Modes** for precise geometry manipulation.

This workspace is commonly used for **creating characters, environments, and props** before moving into texturing and shading.

3. Sculpting Workspace

The **Sculpting** workspace is designed for **digital sculpting** using Blender's powerful brush-based system.

Key Features:

☑ **Dynamic topology (Dyntopo) for adaptive mesh resolution.**

☑ **Multiresolution Modifier for high-detail sculpting.**

☑ **Various sculpting brushes (Clay, Smooth, Grab, etc.).**

☑ **Options for customizing strokes (falloff, spacing, pressure sensitivity).**

This workspace is intended for **organically creating models, fine details, and art sculpting.**

4. UV Editing Workspace

The **UV Editing** workspace is designed specifically for **unwrap and mapping textures** onto objects 3D.

Important Features:

- ☑ **UV Editor for making precise adjustments to UV layout.**
- ☑ **3D Viewport with shaded overlays to be able to view UV maps.**
- ☑ **Intelligent UV Projection, Unwrap, and Pack Islands tools.**

It is used for **game assets, texturing of characters, and visualization of products.**

5. Texture Paint Workspace

The **Texture Paint** workspace allows for painting **directly on 3D models in real-time.**

Main Features:

- ☑ **Painting in the 3D Viewport in real time.**
- ☑ **Brushes for hand-painting custom texture effects.**
- ☑ **Texture Slots for handling various material layers.**

This workspace is utilized for **hand-painting textures, stylized materials, and refining textures prior to rendering.**

6. Shading Workspace

The **Shading** workspace is dedicated to creating and editing **materials and shaders** through Blender's **Shader Editor.**

Key Features:

☑ **Node-based Shader Editor for procedural materials.**

☑ **Live preview of material changes.**

☑ **Compatibility with Eevee and Cycles for accurate shading results.**

This workspace is crucial for **realistic material creation, procedural textures, and PBR workflows.**

7. Animation Workspace

The **Animation** workspace is specifically for **character rigging, keyframing, and motion editing.**

Key Features:

☑ **Dope Sheet and Graph Editor for keyframe management.**

☑ **Timeline for sequencing animations.**

☑ **Pose Mode for rigged characters.**

It is used for **2D/3D animation, motion graphics, and cinematics.**

8. Rendering Workspace

The **Rendering** workspace is where users fine-tune **render settings, lighting, and camera composition** before producing a final output.

Key Features:

☑ **Render Preview for real-time feedback.**

☑ **Camera settings and composition tools.**

☑ **Render Output and Sampling Settings make final tweaks.**

This space promises **highest possible quality output of images and animations.**

9. Compositing Workspace

The **Compositing** space supports **compositing processed rendered images using Blender's compositor node editor.**

Main Features:

☑ **Advanced post-processing special effects in the Node Editor.**

☑ **Mask, color grade, and visual effect tools.**

☑ **Integration with render passes for fine control over final images.**

This workspace is widely utilized for **VFX, green screen compositing, and color grading.**

10. Scripting Workspace

The **Scripting** workspace is designed for **writing and executing Python scripts** inside Blender.

Key Features:

☑ **Built-in Text Editor for Python scripting.**

☑ **Interactive Python Console for testing code snippets.**

☑ **Access to Blender's API for automating tasks.**

This workspace is important for **custom tool, add-on, and automation script creation.**

Customizing Workspaces

Blender provides users with the ability to **custom design and create their own workspaces** according to particular requirements.

How to Create a Custom Workspace:

1. **Click the '+' button** alongside the workspace tabs.
2. Select from **available templates** or use a blank one.
3. Modify the **layout by rescaling editors and adding/removing panels.**
4. Save the workspace to reuse it in other projects.

How to Reset a Workspace to Default:

In case you unintentionally modify something, you can reset a workspace by:
1. Right-clicking on the tab for the workspace.
2. Selecting **"Reset to Default"**.

Why Workspaces Are Important

☑ Task-Specific Organization – Tunes each workspace to a particular task.

☑ Improved Workflow – Reduces useless UI overhead and context switching.

☑ Opportunities for Customization – Lets users create personalized layouts.

☑ Increased Efficiency – Boosts production by keeping the relevant tools readily accessible.

Workspaces in Blender are **an efficient feature that improves productivity and organization.** With proper knowledge of workspaces, users are able to **use Blender more efficiently,** dedicating themselves to creativity and not spending too much time modifying the UI.

We will examine **the Status Bar,** how it helps display system feedback, and how to understand different indicators in the following section.

CHAPTER 6

EXPLORING THE BLENDER STATUS BAR

The **Status Bar** of Blender is a **compact but useful UI element** at the bottom of the screen. It provides **immediate feedback, key system information, and handy shortcuts** that allow users to work more efficiently.

Knowledge of the Status Bar helps enhance workflow since it informs the user about the state of the project at all times, in terms of **performance metrics, operations currently underway, and vital tool tips.**

Status Bar Location and Appearance

By default, the **Status Bar** is at the bottom of the Blender window. If hidden, it can be made visible using:

1. Clicking on **Edit** in the Topbar.

2. Navigating to **Preferences → Interface.**

3. Enabling the **Show Status Bar** option.

The Status Bar consists of several sections that provide **useful system and tool-related information** at a glance.

Components of the Status Bar

1. Active Tool and Mode Information

This section displays:

☑ **The tool that is currently being used** (e.g., Move, Rotate, Scale).

☑ **The current active workspace mode** (Object Mode, Edit Mode, Sculpt Mode, etc.).

This makes it easy for users to see which tool is currently in use and what mode they are operating in.

2. Ongoing Process Display

Blender tends to run background tasks like:

☑ **Rendering**

☑ **Baking**

☑ **Simulation Calculations**

If a process is executed, the Status Bar **displays a progress indicator,** allowing users to track slow process completion.

3. Scene Statistics

The Status Bar displays live scene statistics, including:

- ☑ **Number of objects in the scene** (selected and all).
- ☑ **Vertex count** (useful for modeling and optimization).
- ☑ **Edge and face count** (useful for performance monitoring).
- ☑ **Memory usage** (avoids crashes due to too high resource usage).

Collection | Cube | Verts:8 | Faces:6 | Tris:12 | Objects:0/3 | Mem: 29.7 MiB | v2.81.16

These statistics are of utmost significance for **performance optimization,** especially when working with large scenes.

4. Key Shortcuts and Tool Hints

Blender offers **live tool hints** in the Status Bar, helping the user to understand:

- ☑ **Shortcut keys** for the current tool.
- ☑ **Alternative key combinations** for additional functionality.

For example, when using the **Move tool,** the Status Bar can show:

- **Press X, Y, or Z** to constrain movement along an axis.
- **Press Shift** for precise movement.

This feature helps **newbies learn shortcuts faster** and improves productivity for experienced users.

5. Render Engine and Performance Indicators

During rendering, the Status Bar shows:

- ☑ **Active render engine (Eevee, Cycles, Workbench).**
- ☑ **Number of render samples finished.**
- ☑ **Estimate of time remaining to finish rendering.**

This enables users to **observe rendering performance and adjust settings based on that.**

 6. Error Messages and Warnings
Blender offers **error messages and warnings** in the Status Bar so that users are notified of problems.

Some examples are:
- **"No active object selected"** (when trying to use a modifier without selecting an object).
- **"Insufficient memory for operation"** (in the case of high-res simulations).
- **"File not found"** (in referring to external assets).

Being familiar with these messages helps **troubleshooting effectively.**

Customizing the Status Bar

The Status Bar may be customized by right-clicking on it and selecting:
☑ **Hide or show certain things** (such as statistics or memory usage).
☑ **Reform information to be shown** based on workflow needs.
This enables users to see only the **most relevant information about their projects.**

Why the Status Bar is Significant

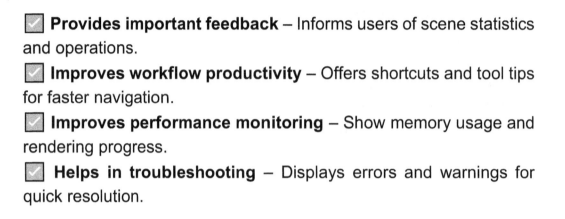

☑ **Provides important feedback** – Informs users of scene statistics and operations.

☑ **Improves workflow productivity** – Offers shortcuts and tool tips for faster navigation.

☑ **Improves performance monitoring** – Show memory usage and rendering progress.

☑ **Helps in troubleshooting** – Displays errors and warnings for quick resolution.

The **Status Bar** is indeed a tiny UI element, but it plays the role of **critical workflow optimization.** Through the tracking of scene statistics, system performance, and tool hints, users can **work smarter and avoid most errors.**

We will now continue to discuss **Areas in Blender,** which help to subdivide the interface into separate functional areas.

CHAPTER 7:

EXPLORING THE BLENDER AREAS AND REGIONS

Blender Areas

The **Blender interface can be highly customized,** which means users can arrange their workspace to best suit their productivity. One of the things that makes this possible is **Areas.**

An **Area** in Blender is a **section of the interface that contains an Editor.** An Area may be **resized, split, or merged** to suit a user's workflow, and Blender's interface becomes very **flexible and customizable.**

Having understood how Areas work, users can **optimize their workspace,** improve navigation, and offer an efficient workflow tailored to their requirements.

Navigating Areas and Their Functionality

1. What is an Area?

An **Area** is a **rectangle area** of the Blender GUI that holds an **Editor.**

Every Area may have:

- ☑ The **3D Viewport** (to model, sculpt, and animate).
- ☑ The **Shader Editor** (to create materials and node-based shaders).
- ☑ The **Timeline** (for animation playback viewing).
- ☑ Any of the **other available Editors** for Blender.

Users can have **multiple Areas** open at the same time, each displaying a different Editor.

2. Resizing an Area

Blender allows users to **resize** an Area by dragging the borders between them.

☑ **How to resize an Area:**

1. Position your cursor on the border **between two Areas.**
2. When the cursor is a **double arrow, click and drag** to resize.

This is convenient when carrying out a range of tasks requiring additional screen space, such as **opening the 3D Viewport to handle complex modeling or widening the Shader Editor to accommodate complex materials.**

Splitting an Area creates **two separate Areas,** and each of them can contain a different Editor.

☑ **Splitting an Area:**

1. Put your cursor in the **top-right or bottom-left corner** of an Area (you will see a tiny diagonal corner marker).
2. Click and drag **towards the middle** to split the Area.

3. Choose a different Editor for the new Area if required.

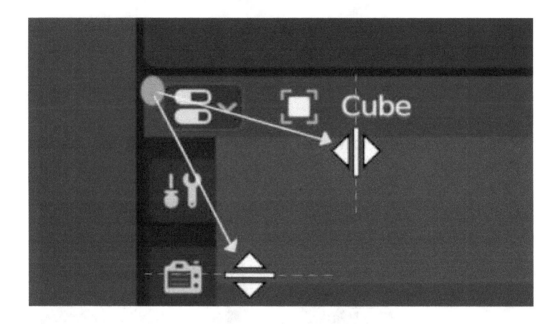

This enables users to **see several Editors at the same time**, for example:

☑ The **3D Viewport** and **Shader Editor** for material design.

☑ The **Graph Editor** and **Timeline** for accurate animation fine-tuning.

☑ The **Outliner** and **Properties Editor** for object and scene property management.

 4. Merging Areas
Merging Areas assists **in clearing out the workspace** by erasing unnecessary areas.

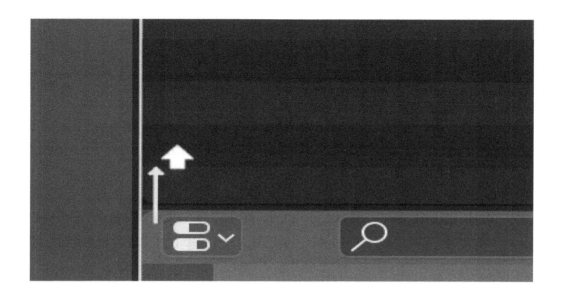

☑ How to merge Areas:

1. Point to the **intersection of two Areas.**
2. Click and drag **into the adjacent Area.**
3. Blender will tell you the direction to merge; release the mouse to accept.

It is convenient to use merging of Areas if you want to **clean your workspace** and have a center for a certain operation.

5. Editor Type Changing for an Area

Each Area can be configured to display a **different Editor.**

☑ How to change an Area's Editor type:

1. Tap on the **Editor Type selector** (little icon in top-left of any Area).
2. Choose a new Editor from the menu (e.g., switch the Timeline to the Dope Sheet).

This feature allows users to **quickly re-organize their workspace** without needing to create new Areas.

General Uses of Areas

- **Two Viewports for Modeling** – One Area to render the **3D Viewport in Perspective mode,** and another one to render **Orthographic views** for precise modeling.

- **Animation Workflow** – One Area for the **Graph Editor**, another for the **Timeline**, and a third for the **3D Viewport** to animate characters efficiently.

- **Shading and Texturing** – A **3D Viewport** to see an advance view of the model and a Shader Editor where materials can be created.

- **Composit Setup** – The **Compositor Editor** to edit with nodes and a **Render Result Viewer.**

Why Areas should be understood

☑ **Makes workflow better** – The users can organize the workspace as per the activity in hand.

☑ **Enhances multitasking** – Allows multiple Editors to be open at once.

☑ **Saves time** – No need to switch back and forth between different Editors.

☑ **Customizable** – Users can design their workspace to fit their personal preferences.

Regions are the **building blocks** of Blender's interface, allowing for a **flexible and customized** workspace. By **resizing, splitting, merging, and editing Editors,** users can create an **optimized layout that enhances productivity.**

We will now address **Regions**, another crucial element of Blender's interface that further streamlines workspace organization.

Navigating Regions in Blender 2025

Blender's **interface is highly modular**, with each Editor further divided into **Regions**. A Region is a **division** of an Editor that contains various UI elements like **tabs, panels, buttons, controls, and widgets.** These Regions help in the structuring of tools, settings, and operations so that it is simpler to work with and workflow efficiency is increased.

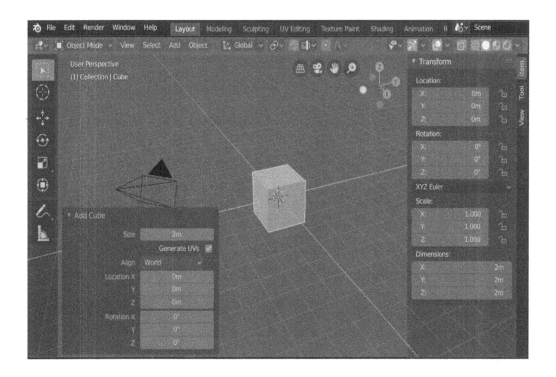

Each Region has a specific function depending on the Editor it belongs to. Some Regions are **always visible**, while others can be **collapsed or hidden** to maximize workspace. Understanding how to use Regions allows users to customize their workflow for greater productivity.

Main Components of a Region

1. Main Region

☑ The **Main Region** is the **main workspace** in an Editor.

☑ These are **main tasks** such as modeling, texturing, animation, or compositing.

☑ Each Editor has its own **Main Region layout,** depending on its purpose.

For example:

- The **Main Region of the 3D Viewport** displays the **scene** to model, sculpt, and animate.
- The **Main Region of the Shader Editor** is a **node-based environment** for material design.

2. Header

The **Header** is a **horizontal strip** at the **top or bottom** of an Editor. It includes:

☑ **Menus** to access different features.

☑ **Buttons** for common tools.

☑ **Settings** that vary with the chosen **Editor type, object, or mode.**

Customizing the Header

- **Right-click (RMB) on the Header** to open a **context menu** with options such as:

Show/Hide Header – Switch its visibility.

- **Show/Hide Tool Settings** – Display tool-specific settings.
- **Show Menus** – Open or close menu options.
- **Flip to Top/Bottom** – Move the Header to the top or bottom of the Editor.
- **Maximize/Full Screen Area** – Expand the Editor to full screen.
- **Duplicate Area into New Window** – Open the Editor in a new window.
- **Close Area** – Combine with an area to its right.

3. Toolbar

The **Toolbar** is located on the **left-hand side** of the Editor and contains **interactive tools** employed for many different purposes.

☑ To **toggle** the visibility of the Toolbar, press **T**.

☑ The Tools in the Toolbar differ depending on the **Editor type and mode.**

☑ In certain Editors, the Toolbar is **editable**, allowing users to customize and re-order or add utilized tools.

4. Tool Settings

A **horizontal band** (like the Header) that contains **options of the current tool.**

Key Features:
- ☑ Located at the **top or bottom** of an Editor.
- ☑ Can be **toggled or moved** with the context menu.
- ☑ Provides **tool-specific settings** (e.g., brush size in Sculpt Mode).

5. Modify Last Operation Panel

This **panel** gives users the ability to **change an operation after a short while of performing it.**

For example:
- After a **Cube** has been inserted, the panel can be accessed to modify its **size, location, and rotation.**
- Parameters like **width and segments** can be adjusted by users after they have performed a **Bevel operation.**

☑ This panel is **context-sensitive,** i.e., it appears only when needed.

6. Sidebar

The **Sidebar** appears on the **right side** of the Editor and contains **object, tool, and Editor-related settings.**

☑ Press **N** to toggle the Sidebar on/off.

☑ It contains **several panels** that are collapsible or expandable.

☑ The content of the Sidebar varies according to **Editor type** and **mode**.

Example use cases:

- In the **3D Viewport**, the Sidebar shows **transform properties (location, rotation, scale).**
- In the **UV Editor**, it shows **UV manipulation options.**

7. Footer

There are some Editors that have a **Footer**, which shows:

☑ **Tooltips** for the currently active tool.

☑ **Shortcut hints** to quickly navigate.

☑ **Live status updates** for some operations.

Example: The **Graph Editor** shows keyframe interpolation settings in the Footer.

Arranging Regions

1. Scrolling

Regions can be **scrolled horizontally or vertically** with:

☑ **Middle Mouse Button (MMB)** – Drag to scroll.

☑ **Mouse Wheel** – Scrolling up/down when the pointer is over a Region.

☑ **Scrollbars** – On timelines and animation editors.

- Certain **scrollbars have zoom control points** so that zoom may be adjusted dynamically by users.

2. Resizing and Hiding Regions

☑ Drag the **border of a Region** in order to **resize** the Region.

☑ **Minimize a Region to zero** to make it invisible.

☑ Hidden Regions feature a **little arrow**—click on it to **show again.**

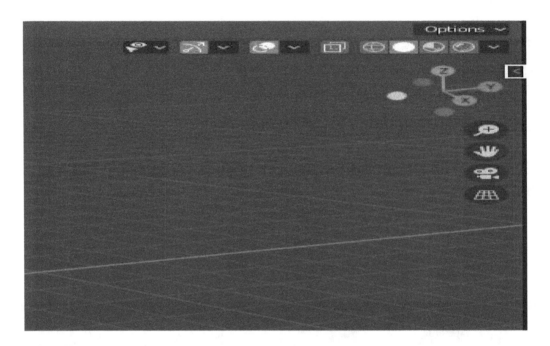

3. Scaling UI Elements

Certain Regions, like the Toolbar, may be **scaled up or down** using:

☑ **Ctrl + MMB drag** – Automatically adjusts UI size.

☑ **Numpad Plus (+) / Minus (-)** – Increments or decreases UI size.

☑ **Home key** – Resets to original scale.

Special Regions: The New Asset Shelf

The **Asset Shelf** is a new feature in Blender that simplifies **asset management** within an Editor.

Key Features:

☑ **Search Functionality** – Use **Ctrl + F** to quickly search for assets.

☑ **Tabs for Organization** – Assets can be grouped into **catalogs**, and these will be displayed as tabs.

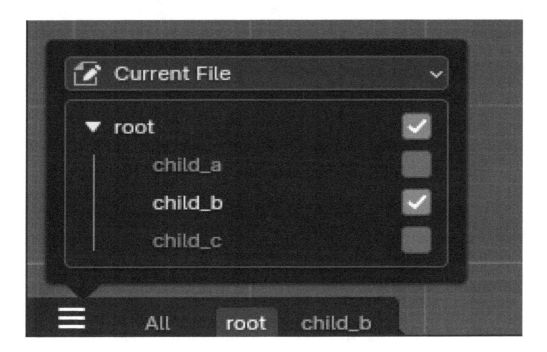

☑ **Display Options** – Control item **size** and switch **asset names** on for better visibility.

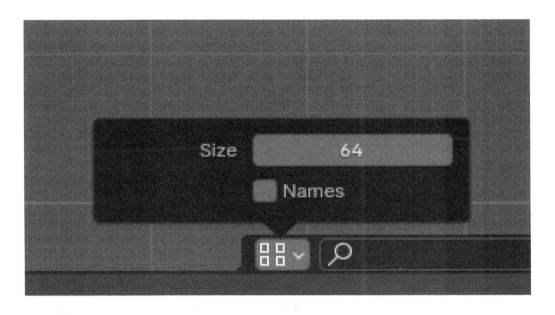

Filtering Assets by Active Tool

- Restricts assets to show only **brushes or tools relevant to the active mode**.
- Filter options are stored in **Preferences** and can be stored manually if **Auto-Save** is disabled.

Why Understanding Regions is Important

☑ **Enhance workflow efficiency** – Easy access to tools, settings, and UI elements.

☑ **Better organizes workspace** – Allows users to tailor their interface for maximum productivity.

☑ **Time-saving** – Eliminates time-consuming switching between Editors and panels.

☑ **Very flexible** – Users can resize, hide, and reposition Regions to meet their needs.

Regions are essential building blocks within Blender's UI that enable users to work efficiently without any hindrance and maintain the workspace organized and within reach. By mastering **Headers, Toolbars, Sidebars, and task-specific Regions like the Asset Shelf,** users can **optimize their workflow** and tailor Blender's UI to suit their liking.

We then explore **Tabs & Panels**, the second element that makes Blender's modular UI even more powerful.

CHAPTER 8

BECOMING ACQUAINTED WITH THE TABS & PANELS IN BLENDER 4.4:

Within **Blender**, the user interface is aimed at being both effective and clutter-free. Among the major building blocks that help achieve this are **Tabs** and **Panels**. These elements of the interface contribute to the smooth accessibility of Blender's functionality with related tools and settings within your reach without hindering the working space.

Tabs: Keeping Your Workspace Organized with Ease

Tabs also assist in wrapping up and partitioning different regions of Blender's interface, and consequently, only a single region would be open at a time. They act in a similar fashion to navigation elements since they facilitate jumping from a category of tools to another without clogging up the screen.

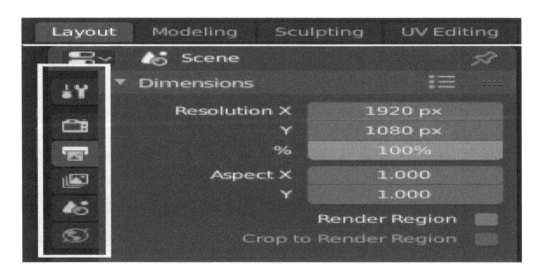

Tabs are contained in a **Tab Header**, which can be **horizontally** (as in the **Topbar**) or **vertically** (as in the **Properties** panel) oriented. The presentation of these tabs varies depending on the current editor.

Switching Between Tabs

Blender has multiple ways of switching between tabs, and switching from one to the next is effortless:

- **Scroll Wheel Navigation:** Pointing to a vertical tab and scrolling using **Ctrl + Mouse Wheel** allows you to move through the available tabs.
- **Shortcut Keys:** Going forward through the tabs is achieved by pressing **Ctrl + Tab,** and going backward is achieved by pressing Shift + Ctrl + Tab.
- **Click & Drag:** Click the **Left Mouse Button (LMB)** and drag the cursor across the tab headers to cycle through the tabs automatically using Blender.
- **Workspace Tabs Exception:** All of the above applies to most of the tabs except **Workspace Tabs** that use a different mechanism and navigation methods all by themselves.

Panels: The Smallest Building Blocks of Blender's UI

Panels are **interactive containers** holding specific settings, tools, and controls. Panels structure features in an editor so related options are accessible in one place for ease.

Panel Structure

- **Main Panels:** The principal areas that store fundamental settings of an editor.
- **Subpanels:** Some panels have additional collapsible parts, known as subpanels, which maintain a clean interface.

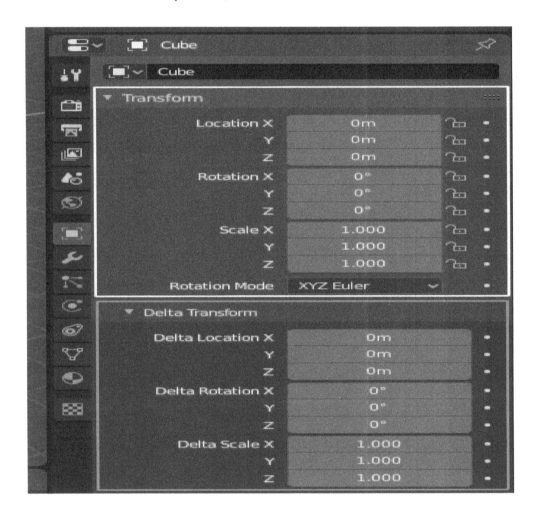

Expanding & Collapsing Panels

In order to maintain the workspace free from clutter, Blender allows you to **expand or collapse** panels dynamically:

- A **collapsed panel** reveals only its title with a **right-arrow (▶)**.

- An **expanded panel** shows all of its tools and settings with a **down-arrow (▼).**

Ways to expand/collapse panels:

1. **Left Mouse Button (LMB) Clicking:** Click on the panel's header to collapse or expand it.

2. **Pressing Keyboard 'A':** Will toggle expanding or collapsing the panel the cursor is over.

3. **Ctrl + Left Click (LMB)** on an **collapsed panel:** Expands it but collapses all other panels in the same group.

4. **Ctrl + Left Click (LMB)** on an **expanded panel:** Expands or collapses all of its subpanels.

5. **Click & Drag Over Multiple Panels:** If you click and drag over a number of panel headers, you can expand or collapse them all at once.

Arranging & Managing Panels

Repositioning Panels

If you wish to rearrange your workspace, you can **move a panel** by:

- Clicking and **dragging the grip widget (::::) on the right side of its header** into a new position in the same editor.

Pinning Panels for Improved Accessibility

There are times that you may **want to have a panel available,** even if you are jumping between different tabs. This comes in handy if you are handling multiple settings at a time, such as setting camera properties as you select various objects.

Pinning a Panel:

- Click on the **pin icon** in the header of the panel to make it remain pinned.
- For panels that have no pin icon, you may **Right-Click (RMB) in their header** and select "Pin" from the pop-up menu.
- Also, you may pin/unpin panels using **Shift + Left Click (LMB).**

Note: Pinning is not available in all sections. For instance, **you can pin panels in the Sidebar, but not in the Properties Editor.**

Presets: Saving & Reusing Custom Settings

Blender has an option to save and load custom settings using Presets. These are particularly useful in applying some settings quickly without having to change each value manually every time.

Preset Menu Options

- **Selector:** Displays available presets for users to choose from.
- **Add (+):** Creates a new preset based on the current settings. A window will prompt you to assign a name to the preset before saving it for future use.
- **Remove (-):** Deletes a preset from the list of available presets.

Presets are particularly handy in **rendering, materials, brushes, and modifiers,** allowing users to have consistency across projects.

Mastering **Tabs and Panels** is crucial in order to easily move around **Blender 4.4.** Tabs are employed for grouping different sections, and Panels provide higher-level settings and controls. Mastering how to turn on/off, pin, and organize these UI components is crucial in order to enhance workflow velocity. Through shortcuts and custom options like presets, users can set up an optimized environment that accommodates their specific needs.

CHAPTER 9:

KEYMAPS AND SHORTCUTS IN BLENDER 4.4

Blender has a number of keyboard and mouse shortcuts that speed up navigation and workflow efficiency. The guide below includes the most commonly used shortcuts and how they interact with different aspects of Blender's interface.

Understanding Shortcut Conventions in Blender

Blender is consistent in some conventions in naming and referring to keyboard shortcuts. The below explains how they have been symbolized throughout this manual:

Keyboard Shortcuts

Single Keys: Keys are merely symbolized as typed on a keyboard. For example, the process of pressing **G** activates the grab/move mode.
- **Modifier Keys**
- **Shift, Ctrl, Alt** – Used in combination with other keys to perform different functions.

Examples of Key Combinations:
- **Ctrl-W**

- **Shift-Alt-A**

Number Keys: 0-9 – Refers to the number row at the top of the keyboard.

Numpad0 to Numpad9, NumpadPlus – For the independent numeric keypad.

Other Keys:
- Special function keys like **Esc, Tab, F1-F12** and the **arrow keys (Left, Right, Up, Down)** are accessed by their names.

Mouse Shortcuts

Blender uses different mouse buttons for selection and interaction:
- **LMB (Left Mouse Button)** – Default for selection of objects and confirmation of action.
- **RMB (Right Mouse Button)** – Toggles context menus.
- **MMB (Middle Mouse Button)** – Used for navigation through the viewport.
- **Wheel (WheelUp, WheelDown)** – Navigates through menus, zooms in/out, or scales values.

Note: There are two supported selection modes for Blender:
- **Left-click select (default)** – More intuitive for users accustomed to other applications.
- **Right-click select** – Offers advantages in workflow efficiency.
- You can alter this preference in **Edit → Preferences → Keymap**.

Shortcut Functions Based on Context

Hovering Over Editable Fields:

When you hover the mouse over an editable field, these shortcuts help you quickly manipulate values:

- **Ctrl-C** – Copy the contents of the field.
- **Ctrl-V** – Paste what has been copied.
- **Ctrl-Alt-C** – Copy a complete vector or colour value.
- **Ctrl-Alt-V** – Paste the copied vector or colour value.
- **RMB** – Pops the context menu where further options will be available.
- **Backspace** – Resets the field to its initial value.
- **Minus (-)** – Inverts the value (multiplies by -1.0).
- **Ctrl-Wheel** – Increments or decrements the value.
- **Return** – Engages pop-up menu options or toggles checkbox options.
- **Alt (while editing values)** – Applies the change in value to all selected objects, bones, or sequence strips.

Animation Shortcuts

Shortcuts are essential to setting and changing keyframes:

- **I** – Insert a keyframe at the current frame.
- **Alt-I** – Remove a keyframe.
- **Shift-Alt-I** – Remove all keyframes of the current object.
- **Ctrl-D** – Assign a driver (to use for automatic animations).
- **Ctrl-Alt-D** – Remove an assigned driver.
- **K** – Insert a property in the current keying set.
- **Alt-K** – Remove a property from the keying set.

Shortcuts for Python Scripting

Blender makes it possible to copy and get Python commands in order to script:

- **Ctrl-C (on an operator button)** – Copies the Python command for that operation.
- **Shift-Ctrl-C (on a field)** – Copies the relative data path (invaluable when scripting and making drivers).
- **Shift-Ctrl-Alt-C (on a field)** – Copies the whole data path of the field.

Dragging Operations in the 3D Viewport

While dragging, rotating, or scaling objects—or adjusting sliders—use these shortcuts for precision:
- **Ctrl** – Snaps the transform to coarse steps (e.g., rotating exactly 90°).
- **Shift** – Blunts changes so fine adjustment is made simpler.
- **Shift-Ctrl** – Snaps to finer steps.

Text Editing Shortcuts

Blender has some default text editing functions for scripting and annotation:
- **Home** – Go to the beginning of the line.
- **End** – Go to the end of the line.
- **Left/Right Arrow** – Move the cursor one character at a time.
- **Ctrl-Left / Ctrl-Right** – Jump the cursor by whole words.
- **Backspace / Delete** – Remove characters.
- **Ctrl-Backspace / Ctrl-Delete** – Remove entire words.
- **Shift + Arrow Keys** – Select text.
- **Ctrl-A** – Select all text.
- **Ctrl-C** – Copy selected text.
- **Ctrl-X** – Cut selected text.
- **Ctrl-V** – Paste copied text.

Confirming & Cancelling Actions
- **Esc / RMB** – Cancel an action.
- **Return / LMB** – Confirm an action.

Shortcuts Customization

Blender offers shortcuts for keyboard and mouse that can be customized by:
Edit → Preferences → Keymap
You can utilize this to customize shortcuts to meet workflow needs.

Default Keymap in Blender 4.4

The default keymap of Blender provides a set of shortcuts that maximize workflow efficiency across various editors and workspaces. This is not a comprehensive guide, but it includes the most common keys in the default setting of Blender.

Global Keys
Global keys are utilized across Blender's interface, affecting file operations, undo/redo, and general navigation.

- **Ctrl-O** – Open an existing file.
- **Ctrl-S** – Save the file currently being edited.
- **Ctrl-N** – Open a new file.
- **Ctrl-Z** – Undo the previous action.
- **Shift-Ctrl-Z** – Redo a previously undone action.
- **Ctrl-Q** – Close Blender.
- **F1** – Access context-sensitive help.

- **F2** – Rename the active object.
- **F3** – Open the menu search bar (convenient to find commands easily).
- **F4** – Open the file context menu.
- **F5 - F8** – Reserved for user-defined actions.
- **F9** – Adjust the last operation performed.
- **F10** – Reserved for user-defined actions.
- **F11** – Display the render window.
- **F12** – Render the current frame.
- **Q** – Quick access to favorite tools.
- **Ctrl-Spacebar** – Enable/Disable Maximize Area (toggles if an editor will expand or shrink).
- **Ctrl-PageUp / Ctrl-PageDown** – Switch to next or previous workspace.
- **Spacebar** – User-defined action (set in Preferences → Keymap → Spacebar Action).
- **Shift-Ctrl-Spacebar** – Play reverse animation.

Common Editing Keys

These shortcuts help object and item management in Blender.

- **X** – Delete the selected item (pops up a confirmation dialog).
- **Delete** – Delete the selected item (no confirmation).

Common Editor Keys

These keys are shared by many editors, including the **3D Viewport, UV Editor, and Graph Editor.**

- **A** – Select all items.

- **Alt-A / Double-tap A** – Deselect all.
- **Ctrl-I** – Invert the current selection.
- **H** – Hide selected.
- **Shift-H** – Hide unselected.
- **Alt-H** – Unhide all.
- **T** – Toggle the **Toolbar** on/off.
- **N** – Toggle the **Sidebar** on/off.

3D Viewport Keys

These shortcuts are only applicable to 3D Viewport operations.

Tab – Toggle **Edit Mode** (Object Mode / Edit Mode toggle).

Ctrl-Tab
- In **Armatures,** toggles **Pose Mode.**
- In other objects, opens a **mode-switching pie menu.**
- 1, 2, 3 **(In Edit Mode)** – Toggles between different mesh selection modes:
  - **1** – Vertex selection
  - **2** – Edge selection
  - **3** – Face selection
- **Hold Shift** – Toggle selection mode but not the rest.
  - **Hold Ctrl** – Change the way the selection is toggled between one and another.
- See **Mesh Selection Modes** for details.
- **Accent Grave (`)** – Open the 3D Viewport **navigation pie menu.**
- **Ctrl-Accent Grave (`)** – Toggle viewport gizmos on/off.
- **Shift-Accent Grave (`)** – Activate **Fly/Walk Navigation** mode.

The keymap of Blender is typically consistent across all platforms, but on macOS, users can use **Cmd** in place of **Ctrl**, with the only exception being system-reserved shortcuts.

- **Cmd-Comma (,) – Display Preferences.**

The default keymap in Blender is geared towards efficiency with fast access to the most commonly used functions. These shortcuts may be customized by users in **Edit** → **Preferences** → **Keymap** to improve their workflow.

Industry Compatible Keymap in Blender 4.4

Blender also contains an **Industry Compatible Keymap**, whose shortcuts are closer to other professional 3D software applications like Maya, 3ds Max, and Cinema 4D. It is meant to be easier to switch to for users from those applications into Blender. The following is a detailed list of the commonly used keys on this keymap.

1. General Shortcuts
These shortcuts control basic operations such as object selection, mode switching, menus access, and quick operations.

- **1 - 3** → Toggles between different selection modes:
- **1** → Vertex selecting
- **2** → Edge select
- **3** → Face select

- **4** → Change to **Object Mode,** so you can edit entire objects.
- **5** → Enables the **Modes Pie Menu,** fast access to an array of interaction modes.
- **Right Mouse Button (RMB)** → Enables the **Context Menu,** which shows typical tools relevant to the selection.
- **Tab** → Enables the **Menu Search,** wherein you can easily locate and make available commands.
- **Shift-Tab** → Fast access to **Favorites**, user-designed frequently used tools.
- **Return (Enter)** → Renames the current item (objects, bones, material, etc.).
- **Ctrl-Return** → Renders the scene, creating a preview of your current work.
- **Ctrl-[** → Toggles the **Toolbar** (helpful for accessing frequently used tools).
- **Ctrl-]** → Toggles the **Sidebar**, which has more object properties and settings.

2. Common Editing Keys

These hotkeys are handy when editing objects, meshes, or any other editable item in Blender.

- **Backspace** → Deletes the selected item **with a dialogue prompt** to ensure deletion doesn't happen accidentally.
- **Delete** → Deletes the selected item without a dialogue prompt (ideal for deleting on a whim).
- **Ctrl-D** → Copies the selected object(s) and pastes an exact duplicate.
- **P** → Toggles the selected object into **Parent** status for another object, creating a hierarchical relationship.

- **B** → Turns on **Proportional Editing** (or Soft Selection), which gives more rounded deformations when you're sliding vertices, edges, or faces.

3. Viewport Navigation

These shortcuts help you navigate the 3D Viewport efficiently.

- **Alt + Left Mouse Button (LMB)** → Rotate the camera around the scene.
- **Alt + Middle Mouse Button (MMB)** → Pan the view, moving it horizontally or vertically.
- **Alt + Right Mouse Button (RMB)** → Zoom in or out.
- **F1 - F4** → Toggles between preset viewpoints:
- **F1** → Front View
- **F2** → Side View
- **F3** → Top View
- **F4** → Camera View

- **F** → Frames the selected object, bringing it to the center of the viewport.
- **Shift + F** → Brings the view to the center of where the mouse pointer is.
- **A** → Frames **all** objects in the scene.

4. Selection Tools

These shortcuts allow to choose objects and components with very high accuracy.

- **Left Mouse Button (LMB)** → Choose an object or component.
- **Ctrl-A** → Choose **all** objects or components for the current mode.

- **Shift-Ctrl-A** → Deselect everything.
- **Ctrl-I** → Invert the selection (choose everything that wasn't already selected).
- **Up Arrow** → Add to the selection (choose additional elements which are connected).
- **Down Arrow** → Tighten the selection (reduce the selection region).
- **Double Left Mouse Button (Double LMB)** → Choose a **Loop** (a series of connected edge or face edges running continuously).
- **Double Alt + LMB** → Choose a **Ring** (collection of edge loops perpendicular to one another).
- **Ctrl + L** → Choose **Linked** objects, such as all faces of an interconnected mesh.

5. Transformation & Tools

These are utilized to switch object transformation and tool mode.

- **W, E, R** → Enable the **Move (W), Rotate (E)**, and **Scale (R)** tools, respectively.
- **Q** → Deploys the **Selection Tools** menu.
- **D** → Enables the **Annotate Tool**, allowing you to draw in the viewport.
- **C** → Applies the **Cursor Tool**, and with it the positioning of the 3D cursor.

6. Edit Mode Tools

All the shortcuts mentioned above, save where they conflict, can be used specifically in mesh object modification when **Edit Mode** has been invoked.

- **Ctrl-E** → Extrudes selected items out to create new geometry.

- **Ctrl-B** → Bevels selected edges to smooth them out through additional geometry added to them.
- **I** → Inserts chosen faces, creating a smaller face in the existing one.
- **K** → Activates or deactivates the **Knife Tool**, which allows for cuts made manually by hand in a mesh with control.
- **Alt-C** → Inserts a **Loop Cut**, creating a loop edge over and over a mesh.

7. Animation Controls

These are used for controlling animation, keyframe setting, and motion data editing.

- **Spacebar** → Play/Pause animation timeline.
- **S** → Adds a keyframe on **Location + Rotation + Scale**, snapping a record of the object's current transformation.
- **Shift-S** → Opens the **Insert Keyframe Menu** for you to indicate which attributes you wish to keyframe.
- **Shift-W** → Inserts a keyframe on **Location** alone.
- **Shift-E** → Inserts a keyframe on **Rotation** alone.
- **Shift-R** → Inserts a keyframe for **Scale** alone.

8. Platform-Specific Shortcuts (macOS Users)

On **macOS**, the **Cmd (⌘) key** can be substituted for **Ctrl** for most shortcuts. However, some combinations of keys are altered due to interference from macOS system functionality.

- **Cmd + Comma (,)** → **Opens Blender's Preferences** menu.

Blender's **Industry Compatible Keymap** is designed for professionals from other 3D software. It provides you with a familiar workflow that feels natural to use but still retains Blender's entire feature set. You can always further customize these shortcuts to your own workflow in **Preferences** → **Keymap**.

With mastering these shortcuts, you will find yourself using Blender proficiently and speeding up your 3D modeling, animation, and rendering workflow.

CHAPTER 10:

UI ELEMENTS OF BLENDER 4.4

The user interface of Blender has a few interactive elements designed to help the user navigate and control objects easily. The elements include **buttons, input fields, menus, eyedroppers, decorators, and a variety of selection tools** to provide the optimal workflow in modeling, animation, and rendering, etc.

This chapter is on **simple UI elements,** discussing how they function and are utilized in Blender.

Buttons

Buttons in Blender serve as the primary means of invoking commands and initiating various features. They come in a variety of forms, each with its own unique function.

1. Operator Buttons

Operator buttons activate **specific operations** when clicked with the **Left Mouse Button (LMB).** The buttons may be displayed in the form of **text, an icon, or a combination of both.** For example:

- **Transform** operations (Move, Rotate, Scale)
- **Rendering** commands (Render Image, Render Animation)
- **Scene-related** commands (Add Object, Delete Object)

Immediately upon the pressing of a button of an operator, Blender triggers an in-house procedure which performs an action immediately.

2. Checkboxes & Toggle Buttons

Checkboxes and toggle buttons are used to **enable or disable options.** Such controls can be enabled or disabled by clicking **LMB**.

- **Checkboxes** indicate an **enabled state with a tick mark (✓).**
- **Toggle buttons** indicate an **enabled state through color changes or icon updates.**

Mass Selection by Dragging

To enable or disable multiple checkboxes or buttons **at the same time,** you can:

- **Click and hold LMB,** then **drag across several options.**
- It works on checkboxes, toggles, and radio button options.

It is useful for doing many changes at once, such as **enabling/disabling a bunch of modifiers or toggling panel settings.**

3. Radio Buttons

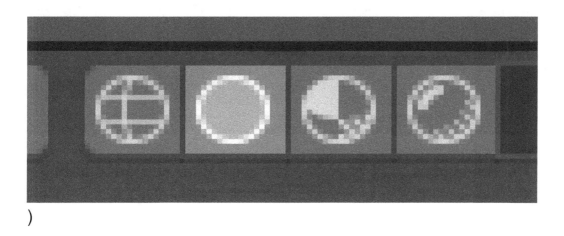
)

Radio buttons allow users to **choose one among multiple options.** Unlike checkboxes, **only one option is available to select at a time.**

- The **selected option** is indicated by a **colored background.**
- Activation of another **involves the automatic deselection of the initial choice.**

Navigation Through Radio Options

Instead of needing to click, you can **scroll radio button options with:**
- **Ctrl + Mouse Wheel** → Roll over the buttons and scroll to cycle through options.

This renders value selection **faster and more intuitive.**

4. Direction Buttons

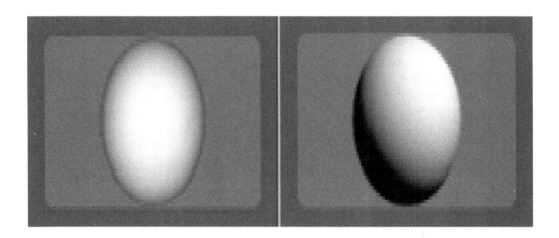

Direction buttons allow users to control **rotation and orientation** by **clicking and dragging** within a circular control. This is commonly applied to:

- Light or object orientation adjustment
- Changing the camera direction
- Setting vector properties for materials

Usage & Shortcuts

- **LMB (drag)** → Rotate direction interactively.
- **Ctrl (while dragging)** → Snap to **vertical** and **diagonal** directions for precision.

This intuitive interface provides precise control over directional properties.

Blender's **UI Elements** form the foundation of working with tools, executing commands, and making selections efficiently. Familiarity with **buttons, toggles, radio selections, and directional controls** will speed up your **workflow**, regardless of whether you're modeling, animating, or rendering.

Next, we have **Input Fields,** another critical component of Blender's UI that allows for precise data input and numerical adjustments.

Input Fields

Input fields are a crucial part of Blender's interface, allowing users to enter and manipulate **text, numbers, colors, and mathematical expressions.** These fields are designed for precision, offering multiple ways to edit values quickly and efficiently.

In this section, we'll cover:
- Text & Search Fields
- Number Fields
- Expressions & Units
- Color Fields

1. Text & Search Fields

Text fields in Blender have a **rounded rectangular border** and may have:
- **Icons** to explain function (e.g., search fields).
- **Pop-up menus** for selecting predefined values.

These fields permit the user to **edit and input text** with the usual text-editing shortcuts. For text fields that also function as **ID selectors**, see the **Data ID section.**

Keyboard Shortcuts for Text Field Editing

- **LMB click** → Open field for typing.
- **Return (Enter) or LMB outside** → Confirm changes.
- **Esc or RMB click** → Abort input.
- **Tab** → Move to the next field.
- **Shift-Tab** → Move to the previous field.

These shortcuts ensure quick text entry, whether renaming objects, setting parameters, or searching for tools.

2. Number Fields

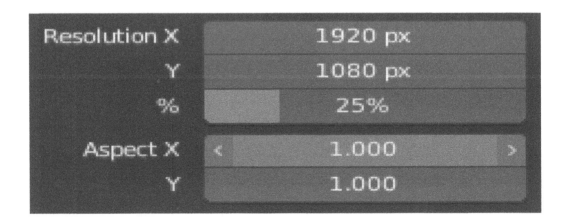

Number fields store **numeric values** and often include **units**. There are two types:

- **Regular number fields** → Display small left (`<`) and right (`>`) arrows for step increments.
- **Sliders** → Feature a **colored background bar** that represents the value graphically along a range (e.g., percentage values).

Ways to Edit Number Fields

A. Incremental Steps
- Once a value is entered, press **Tab** to move the cursor to the next field.
- **Click LMB** on the small arrows (`<` and `>`) to lower/raise values in small steps. **(Impossible for sliders.)**
- **Ctrl + Mouse Wheel** → Move the mouse wheel while hovering over the field to alter values.

B. Dragging for Quick Changes
- **Click & drag LMB** to the left/right to **lower or raise** the value.
- **Ctrl + Drag** → Alter in discrete steps.
- **Shift + Drag** → Enable **precision input** for making precisely controlled adjustments.

C. Direct Keyboard Input
- **LMB Click or press Enter** to directly input a value.
- **Press Minus (-) while hovering** to instantly negate the number.

D. Multi-Value Editing

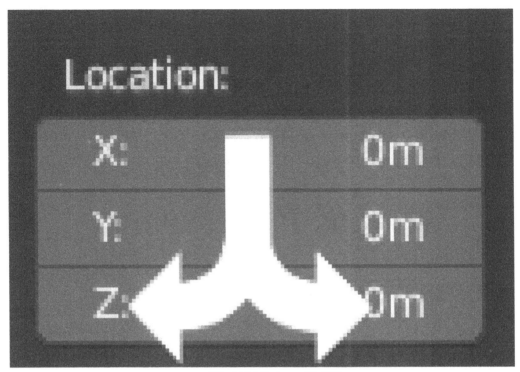

Multi-Value Editing

Blender allows **editing multiple fields in batch** at the same time:
1. **LMB on the first field** and hold.
2. **Drag vertically** over the fields you want to modify.
3. Either **drag left/right** to modify all values **or** release LMB and enter a number manually.

This tool is really useful for making **uniform modifications** to multiple objects, modifiers, or material settings.

3. Expressions & Units in Number Fields

Blender's number fields support **mathematical expressions,** so calculations can be written directly in input fields.

A. Mathematical Expressions

Instead of writing a direct value, you can type:

- `32` → Blender will compute and insert `6`.
- `10/5 + 4` → Blender will calculate as `6`.
- `sqrt(2)` → Computes the square root of 2.

Blender even has constants like **pi (π = 3.142)** and simple functions like `sin()`, `cos()`, and `tan()`.

Python Integration

Blender uses Python to execute expressions. For more advanced operations, refer to the **Math module reference** in Python documentation.

B. Expressions as Drivers

Blender has dynamic expressions with **Drivers**, a part of the animation system.

- Prefixing an expression with (e.g., `frame`) will **create a driver** instead of computing the number only once.
- **Example:** `fmod(frame, 24) / 24` dynamically associates a value with the frame number.

You can also add Drivers using the **RMB menu** for advanced animation control.

C. Using Units in Number Fields

Blender accepts both **metric and imperial units,** and it is possible to combine them within fields.

Examples of Valid Unit Input:

- **Metric:** `1cm`, `1m 3mm`, `2.5km`.

- **Imperial**: `2ft`, `3ft/0.5mi`, `5' / 3\" - 2yards`.
- **Mixed Units:** `2.2mm + 5' / 3\"`.

Blender provides support for **plural forms** (e.g., **meter** or **meters**) and allows you to customize **unit display preferences** in **Scene Settings.**

4. Color Fields

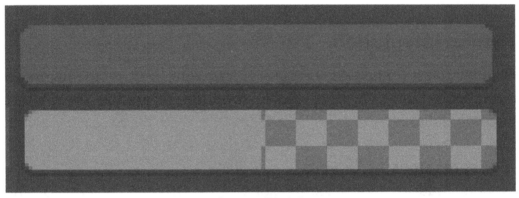

Color Fields

Color fields contain **color values** and offer advanced selection tools with the **Color Picker.**

Types of Color Fields

- **Standard Color Fields** → Display the selected color.
- **Alpha-Enabled Color Fields** → **Split into two parts:**

  - Left part → Shows color **without** alpha.
  - Right part → Displays the color with **alpha** on a checkered background.

- **LMB Click** → Pops up the **Color Picker** for selection.
- **Drag & Drop Colors** → Copies a color from one field to another.
- **Hover Over a Color Field** → Displays a **large preview swatch** with **hex, RGBA, and HSVA values.**

Blender's **Color Picker** includes multiple color modes, allowing users to modify shades, saturation, and transparency with **precision controls.**

Blender's **Input Fields** are feature-rich for typing and editing **text, numbers, mathematical expressions, and colors.** From renaming objects and entering exact dimensions to utilizing dynamic drivers, mastering these controls will **significantly enhance your workflow efficiency.**

Then, we explore **Menus**—another fundamental UI element that organizes Blender's tools and options for **quick navigation** and **efficient access** to commands.

Effective Navigation of Options with Menus in Blender

There are a number of menus available in Blender through which users can interact with tools and operators. Each menu is accessed differently, and it becomes essential to learn navigation of menus for enhancing workflow efficiency through ease of command and preference access. Here is a comprehensive overview of menus in Blender and how you can utilize their functionality to the best.

Interacting with Menus

1. Selection using the Mouse
- Click **LMB (Left Mouse Button)** on the intended menu item to choose it.

2. Number Selection
- Select an item from the list using **number keys** or **numpad keys.**
- Example: **Numpad1** will choose the first item, **Numpad2** will choose the second, etc.

For larger menus:
- **Alt+1** will activate the 11th menu item.
- **Alt+0** will activate the 20th menu item.

3. Using Large Menus
- If a menu cannot be viewed on the screen due to its size, **scrolling triangles** will appear at the top and bottom.
- Passing the mouse over the triangles scrolls the menu up or down.

Menu Shortcuts

To facilitate quicker navigation, use the following shortcuts:

- **Mouse Wheel:** Roll the mouse when it's hovering over the menu.
- **Arrow Keys:** Move up and down through menu items.
- **Underlined Characters:** Press the corresponding letter to choose a menu item.
- **Return (Enter):** Executes and selects the highlighted menu item.
- **Esc:** Closes the menu without selection.
- **Clicking Outside:** If the cursor is moved outside of the menu or clicking outside it, it will close.

Types of Menus in Blender

Blender supports different types of menus based on functionality:

1. Popup Menus

Example of a popup menu in the Image Editor header

- Shows **operators** (operations) which can be executed by clicking with **LMB** or the shortcut indicated by the underlined letter.
- Displays each entry any pertinent keyboard shortcuts that can be used without opening the menu.
- **Quick Search**: Press **Spacebar** and type in the name of the operator in order to find menu items faster.

2. Collapsing Menus

Unchecking "Show Menus" from the header context menu

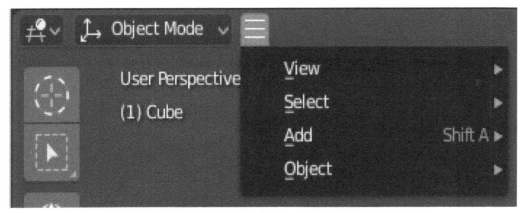

Collapsed menu icon

- Preserves **horizontal space** in the header.
- Uncheck **Show Menus** from the header context menu by right-clicking (**RMB**) on the header.
- Click the collapsed icon to view the menu.

3. Select Menus

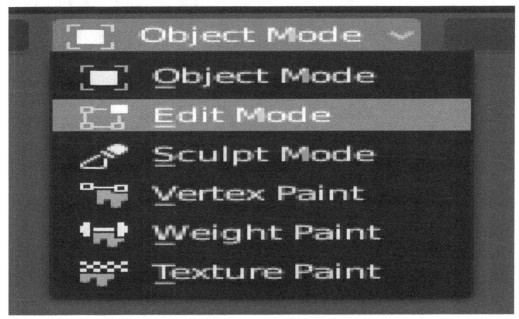

The 3D Viewport Mode Select menu

- A menu of **options** for different settings are displayed.
- Characterized by a **downward arrow** to the side of the menu header.

To use:
- Click **LMB** to open the list.
- Select the desired setting.
- The chosen setting appears within the button.

- Employ **Ctrl + Mouse Wheel** to cycle through selections without opening the menu.

4. Popover Menus

Transform Orientations popover menu

- More like Select Menus but can hold **titles, buttons, sliders, and more**.
- **Usage:** The **Transform Orientations** menu.

Context Menus

These menus give you **location-specific** choices depending on where you right-click **(RMB)** in Blender.

- **Editor-Specific Actions**: Commands vary based on the editor's mode (object mode, edit mode).
- **Property Adjustments:**
  - **Single:** Makes the change to a single value (e.g., X-axis only).
  - **All:** Makes the change to all values in a set (e.g., all coordinates).
  - **Reset to Default:** Press **Backspace** to reset a setting.
  - **Copy Data Path (Shift+Ctrl+C):** Copies the Python path of a property (useful for scripting).
  - **Copy Full Data Path (Shift+Ctrl+Alt+C):** Copies the full context-aware Python path.
  - **Copy as New Driver:** Creates a new driver with this property as input.
  - **Assign Shortcut**: Allows setting a new shortcut to a function.

- **Change/Remove Shortcut:** Change or delete a specified shortcut.
  - **Open File Location:** Opens the directory of the file in the file manager.
  - **Online Manual (F1):** Opens the Blender Manual as a webpage in a web browser.
  - **Edit Source:** For UI developers—opens the source code of an element.
  - **Edit Translation:** Refers to the translation line of code.

Special Menus and Pie Menus

1. Specials Menu
- Works similar to a **context menu** but is triggered by a special button with a **down arrow on a dark-colored background.**

2. Pie Menus

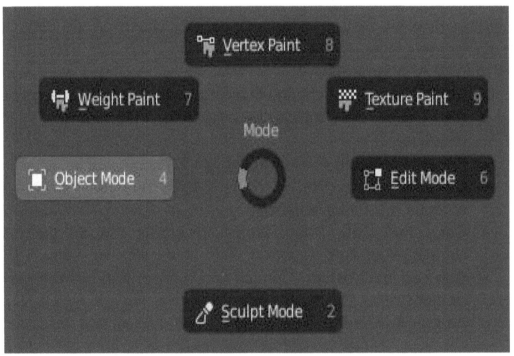

The 3D Viewport Mode Pie Menu

- **Radial menus** in which items are listed in a circular fashion around the cursor.
- Intended for **quick access** to frequently used functions.

How to Use Pie Menus Effectively

- Press and hold the key(s) that activate the menu.
- Gently move the mouse in the direction of the intended option.
- Release the key to execute the selection immediately.
- If you **release the key without moving the mouse**, the menu remains open for manual choice.
- A **disc widget** in the center indicates the current choice.

Key Accelerators:
- Underlined characters indicate shortcut keys.
- **Number keys** can be used rapidly for choice.
- **Sub-menus** are accompanied by a **plus icon** if they exist.

Grasping the menu system in Blender significantly enhances workflow efficiency. Using **popup menus, context menus, or pie menus** and knowing how to navigate these quickly and with ease will overall increase your productivity in Blender.

Eyedropper

The **eyedropper** (pipette icon) allows you to select data from anywhere within the Blender window. The eyedropper can be utilized to select a variety of types of information:

Color Sampling

The eyedropper is used most often for color selection from pixels in Blender.

Note: The **View Transform** setting within **Color Management** affects the sampled color.

- To achieve accurate results, the **View Transform** should be set to **Standard**, or else the eyedropper will provide the wrong color.

Color Ramp Sampling

- When the cursor is dragged across the window, it samples a line, which is interpreted as a **color ramp.**

Object/Object-Data Selection

- You can utilize the eyedropper to choose objects for something like **parenting, constraints, or modifiers.**
- Instead of select from a dropdown, you can click directly within the **3D Viewport** or **Outliner** to choose an object.

Bone Selection

- When setting up a **subtarget** in an armature, the eyedropper can be employed to select a **bone** from the **3D Viewport** or **Outliner**.
- Only bones belonging to the selected **armature** can be selected.

Note: Only in the **3D Viewport,** armature bones can be selected if the armature is in **Pose Mode** or **Edit Mode.**

Camera Depth Sampling

- The eyedropper may be used to sample **distance values** in number fields.
- Another most typical use is setting the **depth of field of the camera,** so that you are focusing precisely on a chosen depth.

Demonstration:
Put a picture of the eyedropper setting the camera's depth of field.

Additional Tips for the Use of the Eyedropper
- **E** – When you place the cursor over a button and press `E`, the eyedropper is activated.
- **LMB Dragging** – Mouse dragging with **LMB** blends colors of multiple points, useful for blending noisy images.
- **Spacebar** – Pressing **Spacebar** resets and starts blending colors once again.

Decorators

Decorators are little buttons that appear as though they're to the right of other buttons, and this indicates the state of a property visually. They are typically found to the side of **number fields, menus, and checkboxes,** showing that the property can **animate**.

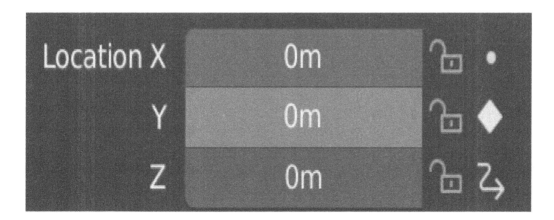

- If the **decorator dot icon** is clicked, it adds a **Keyframe** to the property.
- If the **rhombus icon** is clicked again, it removes the keyframe.
- A **solid rhombus** shows a keyframe on the **current frame**.
- A **non-solid rhombus** shows a keyframe on **another frame**.
- Clicking on a **non-solid rhombus** adds a keyframe on the current frame with the current property value.

Driven Properties

- A property that is **driven** by another is indicated by the decorator with a **driver icon** instead of a keyframe indicator.
- It provides an easier way for users to identify **animated or driven properties**.

Why Use Decorators?

Decorators provide a **quick and intuitive** way to view the state of properties at a glance, enhancing animation workflows.

- **State Colors** – Helps to differentiate between animated, driven, or manually changed properties.

Data-Block Menu

The **Data-Block Menu** assist you in selecting a **data-block** (e.g., a material) so that you can link it with another object. You can use this tool when you wish to handle and reuse assets within a Blender project more effectively.

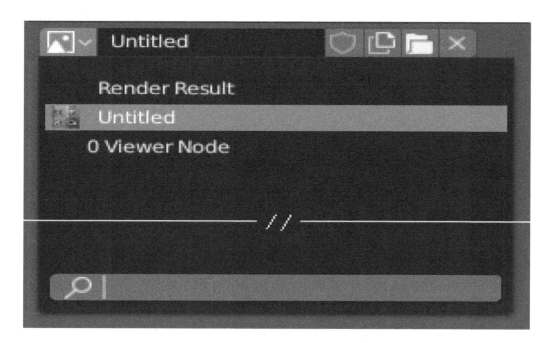

Parts of the Data-Block Menu

1. Type
- Displays an **icon** that indicates the type of data-block.
- The image or the **down arrow** is clicked to activate the **popup menu.**
- You can drag and use the image to apply the data-block to another object (e.g., dragging a material to an object in the 3D Viewport to apply it).

2. List
- Displays **all available data-blocks** in the **blend-file**.
- Some menus also display **previews** of the items alongside their names.

- A **search field** allows quick filtering of items by name.

Note: Data-blocks whose names begin with a period (`.`) are hidden by default.
- To view hidden data-blocks, either **type in a name that begins with `.`** or **select "Show Hidden Files/Data-Blocks"** in Blender's user preferences.

3. Name
- Shows the **name of the current data-block,** which can be modified.

4. User Count
- Shows the number of objects sharing the same data-block.
- A **single-user copy** of the data-block is created when the **user count number** is clicked.

Example:
When **three objects** are sharing the same material, the **user count is 3**.
- **Modifying the material** changes all three objects.
- Clicking the **user count button** for a single object places an independent copy of the content for the object.

5. Fake User (Shield Icon)
- Saves a data-block **not to be removed** even when it has no real users.
- Data-blocks with **fake users** have an **"F"** prefix in the drop-down list.

Example:

- If there are no objects using a material, Blender would normally delete it when saved.
- Select **Fake User** to prevent automatic deletion, so that the material can be accessed on next sessions.

6. New/Add (Files Icon)
- Creates a **new data-block** (or duplicates the one in current use).

7. Open File (Folder Icon)
- Opens the **File Browser** in order to import assets (e.g., pictures for materials).

8. Unpack File (Bin Icon)
- Extracts a **packed file** from the blend-file and stores it as an **external file.**

9. Unlink Data-Block
- **Dissolves the link** between the object and the data-block.
- **Shift + Left Click** reduces the user count to **zero**, which will delete the data-block.

Note: There are multiple functions associated with this icon in other versions of Blender.

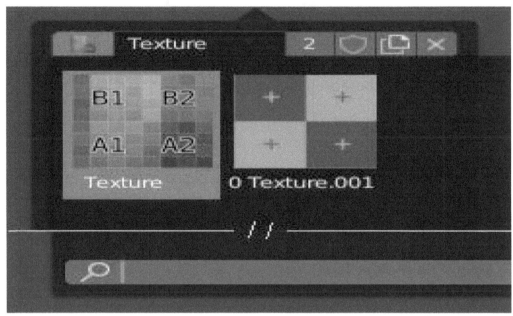

Data-Block menu with a preview of various data-blocks.

Data ID Fields

A **Data ID field** is like the **Data-Block Menu,** but it is employed **solely for choosing** data-blocks—without the creation or administration of them.

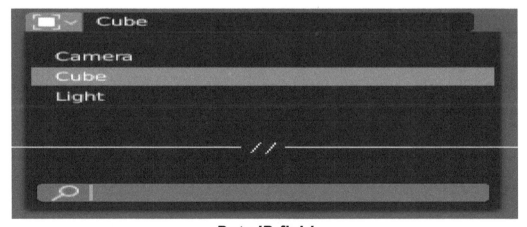

Data ID field.

Components of the Data ID Field

1. Type
- The **icon** on the left indicates the accepted **data-block type.**

2. Name
- The text field serves as a **search field.**
- Press **Tab** to auto-complete names.
- If multiple matches exist, typing further is required.
- Entering an **invalid name** will keep the previous value unchanged.

3. List
- Displays a **drop-down list** of available data-blocks.

4. Eyedropper
- Some **Data ID fields** have an **Eyedropper (pipette icon)** to select objects directly from the **3D Viewport.**

5. Clear Button (X Icon)
- Tapping the **"X"** will empty out the selected reference that is filled with data-block.

6. ID Sub-Data
- Some Data ID fields allow selection of **sub-data types** related to the main data-block.

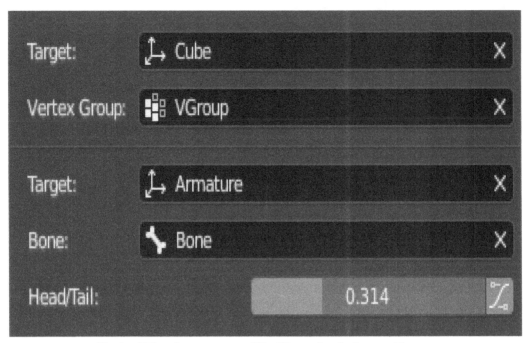

Data-Block menu with ID sub-data options.

Examples of ID Sub-Data Selections

1. Vertex Group
- When the selected **Target Object** is a **mesh** or a **lattice**, a special field is available to select a **vertex group.**

2. Bone
- If one selects a **Target Object** of type **armature**, there is an extra field to select a **bone.**

3. Head/Tail (Bone Positioning)

- If one selects a **bone**, one has the ability to define a point along its length with a **numeric field.**
- `0.0` is equivalent to the **head** of the **bone**, and `1.0` is equivalent to the **tail.**
- Intermediate values **(such as 0.5)** position the selection at a **midpoint** along the bone.

4. Use B-Bone Shape
- If the **bone is a bendy bone,** this setting makes the point move along the curvature of the B-spline rather than stay in a straight line.

Why Use the Data-Block Menu?
- **Link, organize, and reuse** assets in a **Blender project** efficiently.
- **Make standalone copies** at ease when required.
- **Avoid losing unused assets** using the **Fake User** feature.
- Quickly **apply** materials, textures, and modifiers by dragging and dropping them on objects.

List View in Blender

The **List View** control is required to see lists of items in Blender. It has a **main list area,** a **hidden Filtering panel,** and modification buttons to organize entries efficiently.

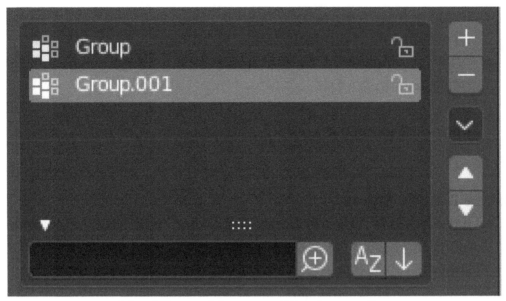

List View with open filtering options.

Key Features of List View

1. Selecting an Item
- **Left Mouse Button (LMB):** Click on an item to select it.

2. Renaming an Item
- **Double-click:** Edit an item's name via a text field.
- **Ctrl + LMB:** Another method to rename an item.

3. Resizing the List View
- **Place your cursor on the resize handle (`:::::`) and drag** to enlarge or shrink the list.

There is no specific selection for renaming an item in the given diagram. It seems the task of renaming an item has been overlooked.

4. Filtering Options

Press the **Show Filtering Options** button (small triangle bottom left) to display additional filtering facilities.

Search (`Ctrl + F`)
- Restricts the list to ones with a given word.

Invert (`<->`)
- Toggles between:
  - **Including** items which match the search term.
  - **Excluding** items that match the search term.

Sort by Name
- **Toggles alphabetical sorting** on/off.

Reverse Order
- Sorts the list in **ascending or descending** order.
- Works with **alphabetical sorting** if enabled.

List Modification Buttons (Right Side Controls)

1. Add (`+`)
- Creates a **new item** in the list.

2. Remove (`-`)
- Deletes the **selected item** from the list.

3. Specials (`v`)
- Shows a **menu with additional operators** to modify list entries.

4. Move (`↑` / `↓`)
- Moves the **selected item up** or **down** in the list.

Why Use the List View?

- Conveniently **work with lists of objects, materials, modifiers, or other objects.**
- Quickly **search, filter, sort, and rename** entities.
- Easy **add, delete, and reorder** members.

CHAPTER 11:

COLOR AND CURVE WIDGETS MANAGEMENT

There are various **color management** and **curve management** tools in Blender that are very essential for compositing, animation, and shading. These tools offer precise management of colors and curves to modify and select color values easily, allowing the users to correct and perfect their work.

1. Color Picker

The **Color Picker** is a floating palette tool that makes it simple to enter a **color value.**

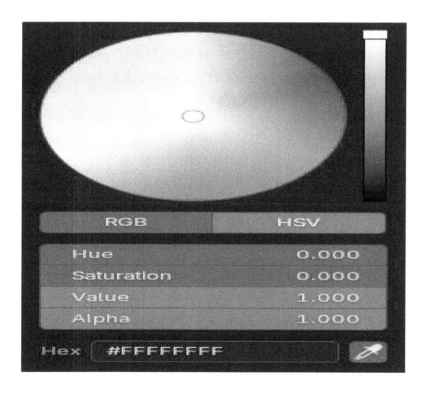

• Picking Colors

- **Ctrl + Drag:** Snaps the hue in 30° increments, making it easier to select **primary colors** (red, green, blue).
- **Shift + Drag:** Enables **precision motion** for more fine-tuned color selection.

• Value/Lightness Slider

- Adjusts the **brightness** of the selected color.
- Fine-tune the **lightness** using the **scroll wheel.**

• Color Models

You can express colors by applying various **models of colors:**

- **RGB (Red, Green, Blue):** The red, green, and blue ones are blended together in order to produce colors.
- **HSV (Hue, Saturation, Value) / HSL (Hue, Saturation, Lightness):** The colors are applied on the basis of **hue, saturation, and lightness/brightness**

• Blender's Color Spaces

- **RGB and HSV/HSL values** within Blender are stored in **Scene Linear color space,** i.e., **not Gamma corrected.**
- **Hexadecimal (Hex) values,** however, **are Gamma corrected** for the **sRGB Color Space.**

> For more on color accuracy, refer to **Color Management** settings of Blender.

2. Color Values in Blender

- **RGB & HSV/HSL color mixing** uses values between **0 to 1.0** instead of **0 to 255** (utilized by most other programs).
- **Alpha Channel**: When transparency is turned on, there is an **additional slider** for the control of **opacity**.

3. Hexadecimal (Hex) Input

- Displays the **hex value** of the selected color.
- Blender supports **shorthand hex inputs** (`dark yellow FFCC00` can be entered as `FC0`).

4. Eyedropper Tool

- The **Eyedropper (pipette icon)** takes colors from **within the Blender window**.

Note: Colors copied with the **Eyedropper** are in **linear color space**, i.e., they do **not account for view transform adjustment.**

- This means picking colors from sample images or background photos **not always yielding as intended,** especially if displayed as overlays.

5. Shortcuts for the Color Picker

Shortcut	Action
Ctrl + LMB (drag)	Snaps hue to **30° intervals**
Shift + LMB (drag)	Provides **precision motion**
Mouse Wheel	Modifies **value/lightness**
Backspace	Restores the value to **default**

6. Color Picker Types

There are different **Color Picker types** in Blender, which are selectable in **Preferences > Interface.**

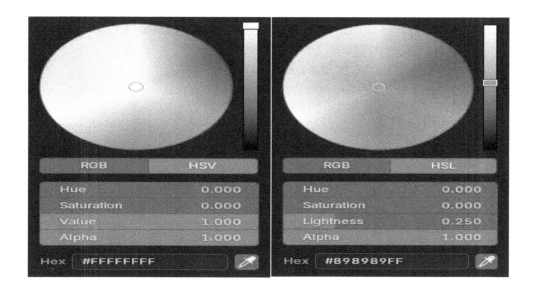

Types of Color Pickers:

Type	Description	Example
Circle HSV	A circle color picker with **Hue, Saturation, and Value**.	**Insert Image**
Circle HSL	Circular color selector by **Hue, Saturation, and Lightness**.	**Insert Image**

Square (SV + H)	Square selector where **Saturation and Value** are managed in the square, but **Hue** is standalone in the shape of an independent slider.	**Insert Image**
Square (HS + V)	A square color picker in which **Hue and Saturation** are set within the square, and **Value** is an alternative slider.	Insert Image
Square (HV + S)	A square color picker in which **Hue and Value** are set within the square, and **Saturation** is an alternative slider.	**Insert Image**

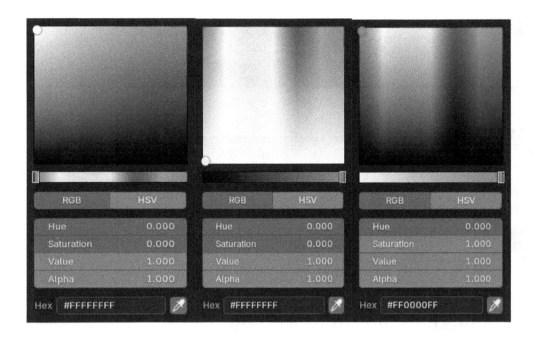

- Provides **precise control** of color.
- Provides **multiple color models** for multiple workflows.
- Includes **shortcut tools** for instant adjustment.
- Includes **Hex input and Eyedropper sampling** to simplify color matching.

Color Ramp Widget

The **Color Ramp Widget** of Blender is an efficient tool used to generate **color gradients** out of a series of **color stops**. The stops determine the way colors shift over the gradient, and the **positions** as well as the **interpolation modes** may be adjusted fine-tuned to achieve precise color shifts.

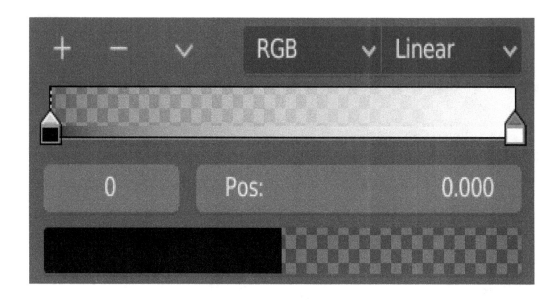

1. Understanding Color Ramps

A **color ramp** is made up of a **sequence of color stops**, each having:
- **A specified position** along the gradient.
- **A specified color** (with alpha/transparency).

Blender interpolates between them to produce a smooth **color gradient**.

2. Color Ramp Controls

Control	Purpose
Add (+)	Inserts a new color stop between the selected stop and the one before it.

Delete (-)	Removes the currently active color stop.
Specials (v)	Provides additional color ramp operations.
Flip Color Ramp	Reverses the gradient over so that all color stops are in reverse positions.
Distribute Stops from Left	Dispenses stops uniformly **from the left side,** convenient for **Constant interpolation mode.**
Distribute Stops Evenly	Gives equal distance between all color stops.
Eyedropper (E)	Grabbed a color from the Blender interface to use on the color ramp.
Reset Color Ramp	Restores the color ramp to its **default setting.**

3. Color Mode Selection

The **Color Mode** determines how colors are combined:

- RGB Mode:
- The colors are combined by **adding** their **red, green, and blue** parts.

- HSV/HSL Mode:
- Colors are converted to **Hue, Saturation, and Value (or Lightness)** before adding.

- This method gives **preservation of better saturation** while transitioning from one color to another in various hues, preventing desaturation (which can happen in RGB blending).

4. Color Interpolation Methods

Interpolation specifies how Blender calculates colors between stops.

RGB Interpolation Methods:

Method	Description
B-Spline	Done with **smooth curve interpolation** for smooth blending of colors.
Cardinal	Used with **soft curve interpolation** with **moderate control.**
Linear	Produces **straight-line interpolations** between color stops.
Ease	Starts slowly, then accelerates and produces a

	smooth **acceleration effect.**
Constant	No interpolation; the color of each stop is **solid** to the next stop.

HSV/HSL Interpolation Methods:

Method	Description
Clockwise	Interpolates **clockwise** around the **HSV/HSL color wheel**.
Counter-Clockwise	Interpolates **counterclockwise** around the color wheel.
Near	Takes the **shortest** possible color wheel route.
Far	Takes the **longest** possible color wheel route.

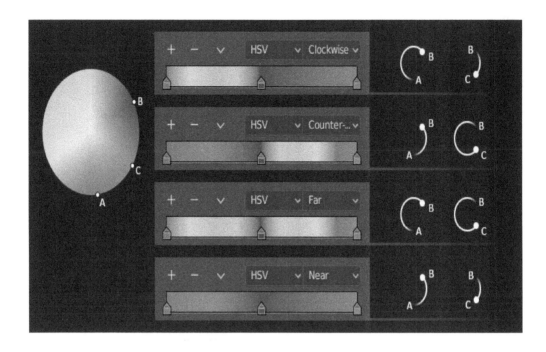

5. Active Color Stop

- The **active stop** is represented as a **broken line**.
  - If stops are **too near** to each other, it might be difficult to click on them. Use the **Active Color Stop Index** to manually select a stop instead.

6. Color Stop Adjustments

Control	Function

Position Slider	Changes the **position** of the current stop on the gradient.
Color Field	Specifies the **color** and **alpha (transparency)** of the stop.

7. Quick Editing Shortcuts

Shortcut	Action
LMB (drag)	Axes a color stop.
Ctrl + LMB (click)	Inserts a new color stop.

Why Use the Color Ramp Widget?

- **Flexible gradient control** for shading, compositing, and texture creation.
- **Multiple interpolation methods** enable precise blending.

- **Supports HSV/HSL color space** for **improved saturation preservation.**
- **Eyedropper and shortcuts** enable faster and more intuitive editing.

Color Palette Interface in Blender: Managing and Organizing Colors for Brushes

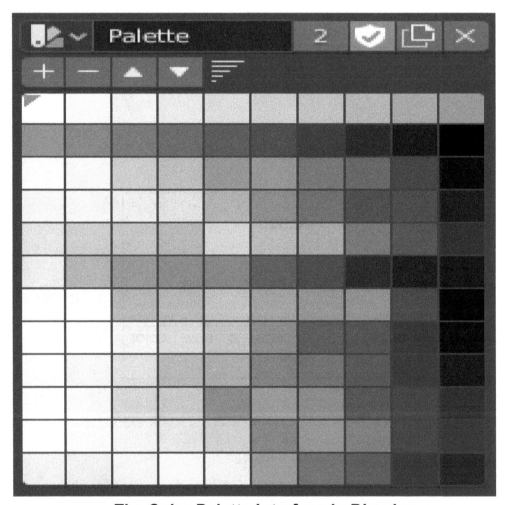

The Color Palette interface in Blender

The **Color Palette** is an essential tool for designers and artists who work with Blender, enabling them to save and manage several colors in an organized way. The tool comes in handy when dealing with complex projects that require the repeated application of colors on different elements. Instead of repeatedly choosing colors manually, users can save frequently used colors in a palette and access them as soon as they are needed.

Whether you are painting textures, vertex color sculpting, or with Grease Pencil, the **Color Palette** streamlines your workflow by allowing you to keep a set of predefined colors, which is easy and accessible.

Palette Management

The core of the **Color Palette** system lies in the **Palette Data-Block Menu,** allowing you to create, manage, and switch between palettes.

Key Palette Controls:

Data-Block Menu:
This is where users select a pre-existing palette or make a new one. Each palette is a container of multiple colors to be utilized at any given moment.

- **New (+):**
Pressing this button adds the **primary color of the current brush** to the palette. This is convenient when working with a particular color

scheme, allowing users to build a collection of most frequently used colors in order to quickly pick from.

- **Delete (-):**

Removes the chosen color from the palette. This helps declutter the palette and only include colors that are needed for a project.

- **Move (↑/↓):**

Allows users to **reorder colors around** the palette. It is useful when arranging colors in a logical manner, e.g., when grouping similar hues together.

- **Sort:**

It provides automatic ordering of colors based on different properties, enabling users to more effectively handle large palettes. Colors can be sorted by:

- **Hue:** Arranges colors based on their position on the color wheel.
  - **Saturation:** Organizes colors from the most intense to the least intense.
  - **Value:** Sorts colors based on their brightness levels.
  - **Luminance:** Orders colors according to their perceived brightness.

These sorting features allow users to effectively organize large sets of colors, granting access to the proper colors immediately when needed.

Color List and Selection

Once colors have been included in the palette, they appear in a **list form** below the Color Palette panel. Each **listing is a visual**

representation of a stored color, and it is quickly accessible and usable on the brush.

- Hitting any of the colors from the **Color List** instantly employs it as the brush's **primary color,** which provides swift transitions between multiple shades and colors when painting or designing.
- This is helpful especially in those operations that require **immaculate color uniformity,** such as character design, company work, or precise textures.

Keyboard Shortcuts for Swifter Workflow

To render the **Color Palette** even handier, there are several helpful shortcuts available in Blender:

- **Ctrl + LMB (Left Mouse Button):**
 Pops up the **Color Picker,** allowing users to instantly change the selected color. **(For further details regarding this, refer to the section describing the Color Picker.)**

- **Backspace:**
Resets the active color to its **default value,** which is useful when you need to revert to an initial color state without manually having to tweak sliders.

Practical Applications of Color Palettes in Blender

The **Color Palette** is used widely in different Blender workflows, some of which are:

1. Texture Painting:

- Having a predetermined **Color Palette** when painting textures onto a 3D model ensures consistency in details and shading.

2. Vertex Painting:

- With the use of palettes through **vertex colors**, artists are able to create color schemes for models without taking time to pick colors each time.

3. Grease Pencil Workflows:

- When creating **2D animations** or **storyboards**, a pre-determined palette speeds up the process and causes characters, environments, and objects to look uniform.

4. Concept Art & Illustration:

- Concept sketch artists can create color palettes that match the project's theme so that designs can be created faster and more harmoniously.

Why Use Color Palettes?

- **Efficiency**: Saves time through providing direct access to colors that are most frequently used.
- **Consistency**: Offers consistency in color usage across projects.
- **Organization**: Helps group and keep colors organized efficiently.
- **Flexibility**: Enables easy modification, sorting, and updating of saved colors.

Customizable Curve Mapping of Input to Output with Curve Widget:

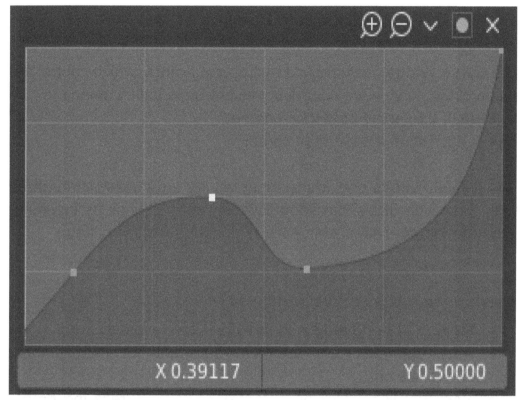

The interface of the Curve Widget in Blender

The **Curve Widget** is a very handy tool in Blender that allows users to manipulate input values and map them to corresponding output values through a user-controllable curve. The tool provides users with very fine control over the modification of data and, as a result, is usable for any number of things, from differing brightness levels while rendering to changing animation easing functions.

The **X-axis** is the input values, and the **Y-axis** is the output values. Users can define how the input develops to the output by modifying the shape of the curve, and it supports both linear and nonlinear mappings.

The **Curve Widget** is controlled by **control points**, which control the shape of the curve. Two control points are provided by default:
- **(0.0, 0.0)** at the bottom-left corner
- **(1.0, 1.0)** at the top-right corner

This default state is one where input values are passed through as such. However, users can set individualized mappings by inserting, removing, or redefining control points and thus modifying them.

Customizing Control Points
- **Move:** Click and drag a control point to relocate it.
- **Add:** Right-click anywhere on the curve with no control point to add a new one.
- **Remove:** Right-click on a control point and press the **delete button** at the bottom right.

Curve Controls: Improving Accuracy

There is a **line of controls** above the curve graph that provides additional functionality to refine and manage the curve.

- **Zoom In (+ icon):** Pushes magnification to the maximum to display greater detail and provide fine tuning. Click and drag in an empty space when zoomed in to pan.
- **Zoom Out (- icon):** Pans out from magnification to view the full curve. Zoom-out capability is limited by the clipping region (below).

Editing & Customization

- **Specials Menu (v icon):** Contains a number of commands for editing control points and curve properties.
- **Reset View:** Resets the original view of the curve graph.
- **Extend Options:** Controls what happens to the curve before the first control point and after the last.

Extend Options:
- **Extend Horizontal:** The curve is horizontal prior to the first point and subsequent to the last point.

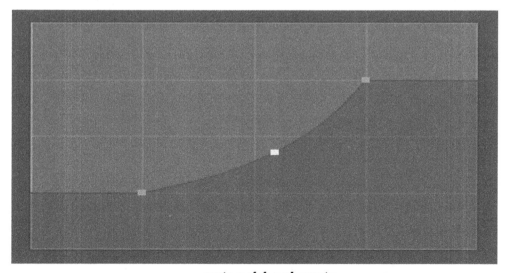

extend-horizonta

- **Extend Extrapolated:** The curve extends along its existing trend prior to the first point and subsequent to the last point, based on its overall shape.

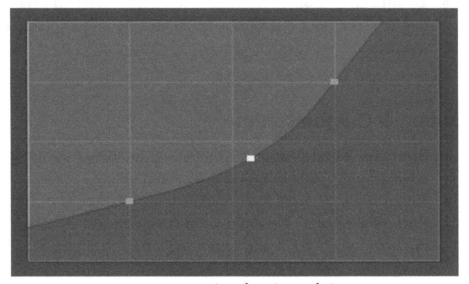

curve extend-extrapolate

- **Reset Curve:** Removes all additional control points, bringing the curve back to its initial linear form.

Clipping Options: Setting Limits

The **Clipping Options** (dot icon) allow users to restrict the control points of the curve within a specified range.

- **Use Clipping:** Limits all control points to stay within specified limits.
- **Min X/Y & Max X/Y:** Determines the minimum and maximum values for control point placement on both axes.

This avoids output values passing a certain value, useful when working within defined limits, such as brightness levels or motion control.

Handle Types: Controlling Curve Interpolation

Each control point has **Handle Types** to specify the type of how it influences the form of the curve. To smooth or jerky transitions of mapped values is what this is done for.

Handle Types:
- **Vector Handle:** Constructs straight-line segments, and sharp angles exist.

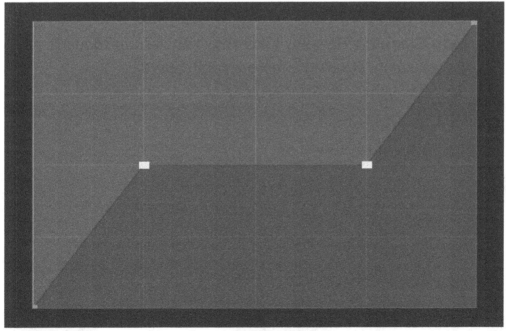

handle-vector

- **Auto Handle:** Creates automatically smooth curves in between points.

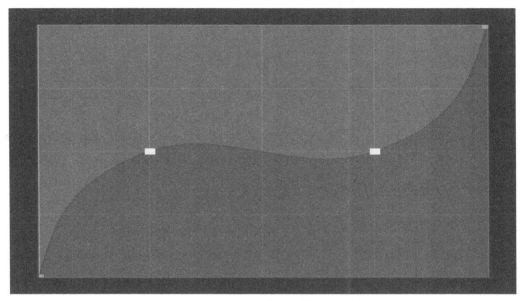

curve handle-auto

- **Auto-Clamped Handle:** Like auto handles but doesn't allow overshooting, creating a more smooth curve.

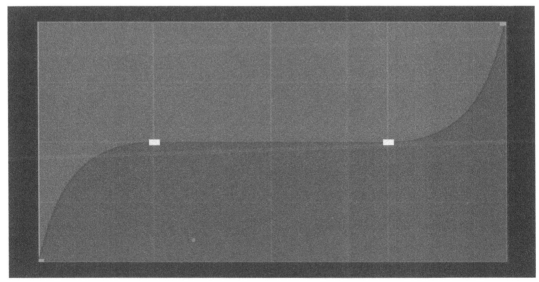

curve handle auto clamped

Free Handle: Puts the handles free from any restrictions, which allows them to change direction in a jerky manner.

- **Aligned Free Handles:** Prevents both handles of a point from ever getting away from being opposite each other, which makes the curves appear smooth.

Modifying Handle Types:

Users can switch between one handle type and another to achieve the desired effect by choosing a control point and altering its handle type through the properties panel.

Extra Functions

- **X, Y Coordinates:** Shows the exact position of a selected control point to position it accurately.
- **Delete**: Removes the selected control point (first and last points cannot be deleted).
- **Copy/Paste (Ctrl + C / Ctrl + V):** Allows users to copy a curve from one **Curve Widget** and paste it into another. Simply move the mouse over the curve and use the shortcut keys.

Practical Applications of the Curve Widget

The **Curve Widget** is widely utilized in numerous Blender workflows, including:

1. **Shader Adjustments:** Color ramp adjustments, brightness, and contrast.

2. **Animation Easing:** Customizing animation transitions and speed changes.

3. **Grease Pencil Effects:** Controlling Grease Pencil line thickness and transparency.

4. **Physics & Simulations:** Setting input forces to output simulations.

5. **Audio Waveforms:** Softening or amplifying sound volume and effects in animation projects.

By learning the **Curve Widget**, users have at their disposal a powerful tool for managing and tweaking transformations, animations, and procedural effects in Blender.

CHAPTER 12:

TOOLS AND OPERATORS

Blender possesses an entire system of interactive tools and operators that are intended to perform various editing operations in a simple way. The tools and operators are utilized by the users to change objects, scenes, and many other things into accurate and controllable forms. The following are what this chapter includes:

- **Tool System** – An overview of Blender's interactive tools and how they work.
- **Operators** – A guide of the commands used in scene and object editing.
- **Undo & Redo** – Instructions on how to undo and edit changes effectively.
- **Annotations** – A feature by which users are allowed to enter comments, sketches, or annotations inside Blender.

Tool System

Tools for Blender are presented in the **Toolbar,** providing a structured way of accessing and manipulating objects based on the current workspace and mode of editing. Only a **single active tool is permitted for each workspace at any one time,** and Blender maintains this selection when switching between different modes.

For instance, when you are in **Edit Mode** and have the **Extrude Tool** active and then go to **Object Mode,** where extrusion is not supported, Blender will keep the **Extrude Tool** when you come back to **Edit Mode.** This keeps the smooth workflow without having to continuously select tools.

All but a few tools are activated with the **Left Mouse Button (LMB),** but some require one or more modifier keys (such as **Shift**, **Ctrl, or Alt),** which are identified in the **Status Bar** while using the tools. User interface for tool interaction can also be personalized by users through the **Keymap Preferences.**

Some tools also include **gizmos** (such as **Shear and Spin),** providing an interactive graphical interface to set tool parameters.

Accessing the Toolbar

- **Shortcut:** `T`
  - **Location:** Displayed on the left side of the workspace.

The **Toolbar** holds the buttons for various tools, a few of which are organized in groups. The groups of tools are indicated by a **small triangle** in the bottom-right corner of the button. Clicking and holding **LMB** on the buttons will show the expanded group of tools. Dragging **LMB** across the button will also immediately open the group.

  - **Tooltips:** Hovers over an icon briefly reveal the name of a tool, and a lengthy hover triggers a more detailed tooltip containing more information.

- **Toolbar Resizing:** Horizontal toolbar width expands icons to **two groups,** and more expansion displays icons and text names for better readability.

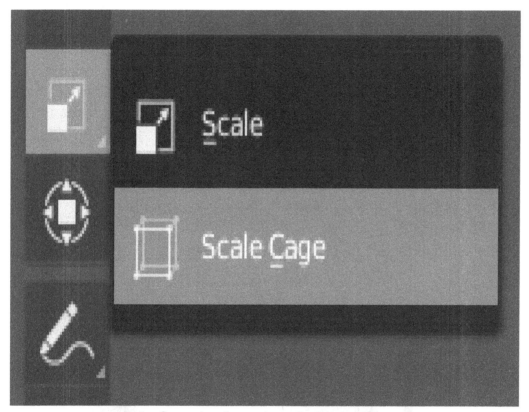

Interface tool system buttons popup

Expanded toolbar group interface presenting several tools inside a category.

Pop-Up Toolbar

- **Shortcut:** `Shift + Spacebar`

- **Function:** Activates a floating toolbar close to the cursor to access tools faster.

This enables users to **change tools quickly without going to the main toolbar.** The tool is presented along with its shortcut for ease of reference.

Also, users can assign **Spacebar** as a modifier key in the **Keymap Preferences** to activate tools using key combinations. That is, for instance:
- `Spacebar + T` → **Transform Tool**
- `Spacebar + D` → **Annotate Tool**
- `Spacebar + M` → **Measure Tool**

This setting provides a convenient and dynamic way of accessing frequently used tools.

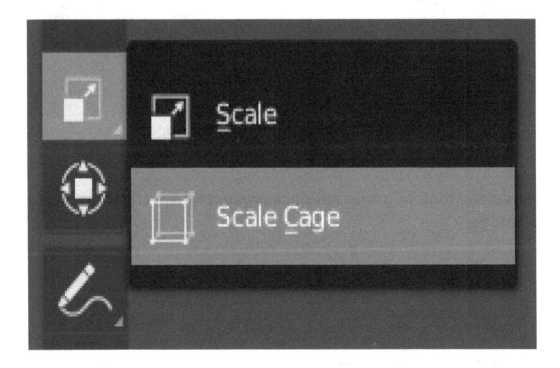

Quick Favorites Menu

- Shortcut: `Q`
- **Function:** Customizable menu for quick access to most frequently used tools.

The **Quick Favorites** menu enables users to add tools or menu items for **faster access** in workflow. Items can be added by right-clicking on a tool and selecting **"Add to Quick Favorites."**

Switching Tools

Alt Click Tool Prompt
- **When activated** under **Keymap Preferences,** pressing `Alt` displays a **tool selection prompt** on the Status Bar.
- **An associated key** may be pressed to select a tool, or `Alt` may be pressed again to dismiss the prompt.

Fallback Tool
- The **fallback tool** is the currently active tool if none is actively chosen.
- It is the **leading tool** found at the very top of the **Toolbar.**
- Users may alternate it by:
  - Pressing and holding **LMB** over the toolbar button.
  - Pressing `Alt + W` to provide a **pie menu** where selection is allowed.

Cycling Between Tools
- If a shortcut key is pre-assigned to a collection of tools, having the Cycle feature enabled within the Keymap Editor allows individuals to cycle through tools in a group with the same key pressed over and over.

- In the 3D Viewport, this works for the selection tools:
  - The **W** key pressing cycles through **Select Box, Select Circle,** etc.

Tool Properties and Settings

Each tool comes with **configurable settings,** accessible from multiple locations:

1. **Sidebar (`N` Key)** → Under **Tool** → **Active Tool Panel**
2. **Properties Editor** → **Active Tool Tab**
3. **Tool Settings Panel** → Located below the area header in the workspace

These options allow users to **fine-tune** tool actions for more precision in editing.

Summary of Key Shortcuts for Tool System

Table Showing Summary of Key Shortcuts for Tool System

Action	Shortcut Key

Show/Hide Toolbar	`T`
Open Pop-Up Toolbar	`Shift + Spacebar`
Open Quick Favorites	`Q`
Select Fallback Tool	`Alt + W`
Cycle Through Tools	Key assigned (e.g., `W` for Selection Tools)

Blender Operators

Operators in Blender are instructions that execute an operation as soon as they are activated. Operators do not require human input or intervention like tools. Operators begin their work instantly after activation. These operations are the foundation of Blender operations that allow objects to be modified, values adjusted, and processing of different operations in the scene.

The operators can be activated in more than one way:
- **Operator Buttons:** Found in different panels and menus.
- **Popup Menus:** Quick-access menus for specific functions.

- **Menu Search:** A searchable interface for finding and executing commands.

Common examples of operators include:
- Adding or deleting objects
- Changing shading modes (e.g., smooth or flat shading)
- Transforming objects instantly

Operator Properties

Most operators have parameters that can be tweaked to precision their output. An operator initially works with its preset properties, but the users can further tweak the outcomes using the help of the Adjust Last Operation panel. The panel automatically opens when operating an operator to allow users to tweak parameters such as scale, rotation, and position.

Modal Operators

Modal operators are a mixture of tools and normal operators. They require interactive input before performing an action. Modal operators allow users to finalize changes in real time before committing or canceling the action.

- **Committing a Modal Operator:**
  - **LMB (Left Mouse Button)** or **Return (Enter)** commits the action.

- **Canceling a Modal Operator:**

- **RMB (Right Mouse Button)** or **Esc (Escape)** cancels the operation.

Examples of modal operators include:
- Transform adjustments (move, scale, rotate)
- Beveling edges in Edit Mode
- Sculpting operations with dynamic brush controls

Slider Operators

Slider operators allow users to modify an **percentage value** interactively in the **Header** of an editor. Sliders provide a convenient way of modifying values with instant feedback.

How to Modify a Slider Operator:

- **Drag Left or Right:** Modifies the value smoothly.
- **Hold Ctrl:** Gives snapping in **10% increments** for quick modifications.
- **Hold Shift:** Provides finer, more accurate control over values.
- **Press E:** Puts "overshoot mode" into effect so values can be moved beyond the normal 0-100% range.

Fine control over setting such as opacity, strength, and intensity for most tools is made available by this interactive design.

Finding Operators

There are powerful search options in Blender that help users to find and use operators easily.

Menu Search
- **Mode**: All modes
- **Location**: `Edit` → `Menu Search`
- **Shortcut**: F3

The **Menu Search** dialog allows users to search for specific operators within Blender's user interface. Users can type a part of the name of an operator to narrow down results and execute the target command by:
- Clicking on it with **LMB**
- Navigating using **Up/Down arrows** and pressing **Return**

This aspect also indicates the **position of the menu** where the operator is, hence it is easier to find it for the future.

Operator Search in Action Example:

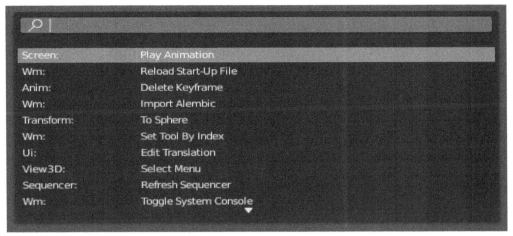

operator search pop-up

The Operator Search pop-up displaying operator suggestions.

Operator Search (Developer Mode)

- **Mode:** Compatible with all modes
- **Position:** `Edit` → `Operator Search`

For developers and power users, Blender provides an **Operator Search** option, accessible when **Developer Extras** are enabled. The search function is more complete than the standard **Menu Search,** which shows all the operators available to access, including those not in the standard menu system.

Benefits of Operator Search:
- Easy for Python developers to try new functions
- Helps discover advanced operators not available via standard menus
- Enables quick execution of master commands

Blender also offers users the option to customize how search results are displayed in the **User Preferences**. This offers a more personalized workflow when using the search function.

For further customization, users can also modify the **Spacebar Action** in Preferences to launch either **Tool Search** or **Menu Search** based on their workflow preference.

Undo & Redo in Blender

There are robust **Undo & Redo** features available in Blender that support users in recovering from errors, fine-tuning their operations, and moving through their edit history. They help users do the following:

- **Undo** the previous action
- **Redo** a previously undone action
- Modify the last operation's parameters
- View an undo history list
- Repetition of previous operations

Undo (Ctrl + Z)

- **Mode**: Available in all modes
- **Menu Location:** `Edit` → `Undo`
- **Shortcut: Ctrl + Z**

Undoing an action in Blender is as simple as pressing **Ctrl + Z**. This function allows users to roll back their most recent change, making it an essential tool for correcting mistakes and refining work.

Tip: Users can configure undo settings under **Preferences** → **Memory & Limits** to adjust how many undo steps Blender stores.

Redo (Shift + Ctrl + Z)

- **Mode:** Available in all modes
- **Menu Location:** `Edit` → `Redo`
- **Shortcut: Shift + Ctrl + Z**

Redo reverses the **Undo** operation, allowing users to step forward through changes they previously undid. This is useful when experimenting with modifications and needing to switch between different states.

Adjust Last Operation (F9)

- **Mode**: Available in all modes
- **Menu Location**: `Edit` → `Adjust Last Operation…`
- **Shortcut: F9**

Adjust Last Operation.

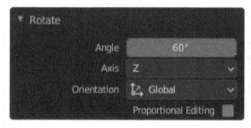

Rotation (Object Mode, 60 degrees).

Scale (Edit Mode, Resize face).

After the execution of an operator, users can further refine the properties of the operator through the use of the **Adjust Last Operation** panel. The panel is located in the **bottom-left corner** of the editor or accessible with F9. Users can then set some parameters like:

- **Rotation Angle** for transformations;

198

- **Scale and Position** for objects and faces;
- **Number of Vertices** for added primitives;

Example Usage:
- If a user **rotates an object**, the panel will show the **rotation angle** so that it can be adjusted fine.
- If a user **adds a circle**, they can adjust the **vertex count** straight away to make it a triangle or polygon.

Tip: If the panel is not visible, toggle it on through `View` → `Adjust Last Operation`.

Undo History

- **Mode:** Present in all modes
- **Menu Location:** `Edit` → `Undo History`

Blender records a **history** of actions, allowing users to jump to a specific point instead of stepping back one action at a time.

How to Use Undo History:

1. Open the **Undo History** menu (`Edit` → `Undo History`).
2. Select any previous action from the list.
3. Blender will revert the project to that exact state.

Important Notes:
- The **most recent actions** are at the top of the list.
- A **dot** indicates the **current position** in the history.
- Once a new action is performed, all future history steps **are erased** from that point.

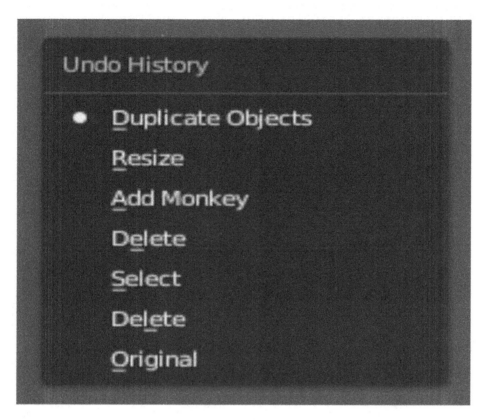

The Undo History menu displaying past actions.

Repeat Last Action (Shift + R)

- **Mode**: Available in all modes
- **Menu Location:** `Edit` → `Repeat Last`
- **Shortcut: Shift + R**

The **Repeat Last** function allows users to instantly redo the most recent action without needing to go through menus or reconfigure settings.

Example:

1. **Duplicate an object** (e.g., press `Shift + D` to duplicate a monkey mesh).
2. Move the duplicated object slightly.
3. Press **Shift + R** to duplicate and move it again.

This feature is extremely useful for repetitive tasks such as:
- Duplicating objects with consistent spacing
- Applying transformations multiple times

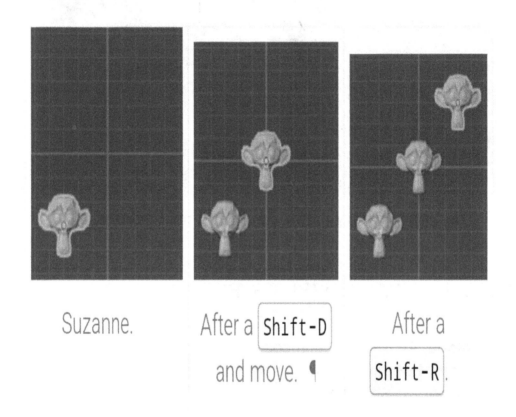

Suzanne. After a `Shift-D` and move. ❪ After a `Shift-R`.

Suzanne (Monkey mesh) before and after repeating the last action.

Repeat History

- **Mode**: Available in all modes
- **Menu Location:** `Edit` → `Repeat History`

Blender also records a history of **repeated** actions. Unlike **Undo History**, which stores all actions, **Repeat History** only logs actions that have been executed multiple times.

How to Use Repeat History:

1. Open the **Repeat History** menu (`Edit` → `Repeat History`).
2. Select any action from the list.
3. Blender will repeat the selected action.

The Repeat History menu showing previously repeated actions.

- When quitting Blender, the entire **action history is lost,** even if the file is saved.

- If an action is repeated from history, it retains its previous parameters.

Blender's **Undo & Redo** system is a crucial tool for efficient workflow management. Whether correcting mistakes, fine-tuning operations, or automating repetitive tasks, these functions ensure a seamless editing experience. Users can maximize productivity by mastering:

- **Ctrl + Z** for Undo
- **Shift + Ctrl + Z** for Redo
- **F9** for Adjusting the Last Operation
- **Undo History** for timeline navigation
- **Shift + R** for repeating the last action

By leveraging these tools, Blender users can experiment freely and optimize their creative process.

Annotations in Blender 4.4

Blender's **Annotation Tool** offers the capacity to insert notes and visual marks right on objects, node configurations, or 2D images. It is useful for making fast sketches, marking important details, or collaborating with colleagues. Annotations are present in a variety of editors, and they behave similarly to digital handwriting tools.

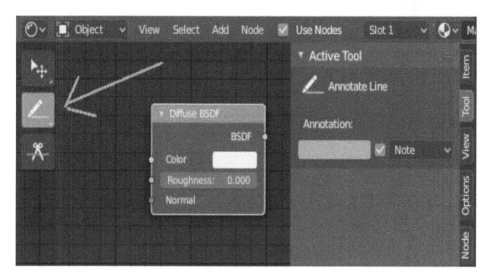

Annotations tool in a node editor.

Types of Annotation Tools

The annotation tool can be accessed from the **Toolbar**, and it comes with several sub-tools:

1. **Annotate (Freehand Drawing)**
   - This tool allows users to draw freehand strokes in the active editor.

2. **Annotate Line**

   Click and drag to create straight lines.
   - Different **arrow styles** for the line beginning and end can be chosen by users.

3. **Annotate Polygon**
   - Double click to create a **sequence of adjacent straight lines.**
   - Press **Enter (Return) or Esc** to complete the drawing.

4. Annotate Eraser

To erase annotation strokes drawn.

- The **eraser radius** can be adjusted in the **Tool Settings.**

Annotation Tool Settings

There are a number of settings that control how annotations will act and appear:

1. Color

- Users can be compelled to adjust the color of **new as well as existing** annotation strokes.

2. Annotation Layer

- A menu with the **active annotation layer**, allowing users to have numerous layers.

3. Placement Options

The **Placement** option controls where the annotations are rendered:

- 3D Cursor (3D Viewport Only)

- Strokes are rendered in 3D space on an **imaginary plane** that is parallel to the 3D Cursor.

- Surface (3D Viewport Only)

- Strokes are drawn **on the surface of objects** directly.
- If there is no object, this acts like the **3D Cursor** placement.

- Image (2D Editors Only)

- Annotations are drawn **on 2D images** directly in the **Image Editor** or other 2D areas.
- Their location scales dynamically with zoom and pan.

- View

- **Annotations are fixed on the screen**, i.e., they do not move when the viewport is rotated, panned, or zoomed.

4. Advanced Placement Settings
- **Only Endpoints Surface Placement** → Snaps only the **start and end points** of the stroke onto a surface.
- **Project Onto Selected Surface Placement** → Annotations will **only appear on selected objects.**

5. Stabilize Stroke
- Assists with the drawing of smoother lines by **reducing jitter.**
- Adjustable settings:
  - **Radius** → Minimum distance before resuming a stroke.
  - **Factor** → A control smoothing factor that hesitates to place a stroke for more control.

6. Annotate Line Styles
- Users can modify the **start and end ornaments** of lines (e.g., adding arrowheads).

Managing Annotation Layers

Blender has support for creating and managing multiple layers of annotations in order to further organize your work. The settings are located in:

Sidebar → View → Annotations Panel

Layer Control
- Opacity → This controls the strokes to be more or less transparent. Thickness → This changes the thickness of the stroke.

- **Onion Skinning** → Displays faded out versions of strokes from **past and upcoming frames**, useful in animation workflows.

Onion Skinning Settings

- **Before/After Colors** → Determines colors for past and upcoming frames.
- **Frame Range** → Determines how many frames to display before and after the current one.

Note: Onion Skinning only works in the 3D Viewport and the Sequencer.

- The **Annotation Tool** of Blender is ideal to add quick marks, drawings, and annotations.
- A person can choose among **freehand, straight line, or polygon** annotation types.
- Annotations can be located in **3D space, on objects, images, or stuck on the screen.**
- **Fine-tuned settings** like the stabilization of stroke and **Onion Skinning** make the process more precise.

CHAPTER 13:

SELECTING AND MANIPULATING OBJECTS IN BLENDER 4.4

Selecting is one of the most basic operations in Blender and constitutes the foundation of modeling, animation, and scene manipulation. No matter what you are doing with objects, vertices, edges, or faces, knowledge of selecting techniques enhances workflow speed and precision. In addition, Blender's node-based approach relies on selecting and arranging to construct complex workflows.

In this chapter, different selection methods and manipulation techniques are explained, e.g., working with nodes, node elements, and organizational tools that make the workflow more readable.

Definition of Terms

1. Selecting in Blender
Selection is the process of choosing objects or items in Blender to apply transformations or edits to them. There are different selection tools in Blender, each used for different reasons.

1.1 Selecting Objects

By default, Blender uses **Left Mouse Button (LMB)** for selection, but this can be changed in the Preferences. The following selection tools can be used:

- **Tweak Selection (Shortcut: W**): Click or drag to select and move an object.
- **Box Selection (Shortcut: W):** Click and drag a rectangle to select multiple objects.
- **Circle Selection (Shortcut: W):** Click and drag a circular selection area.
- **Lasso Selection (Shortcut: W):** Select by drawing freely around objects.

Holding **Shift** while selecting adds objects to the selection, and **Ctrl** removes them.

1.2 Selecting Components (Vertices, Edges, and Faces)
In **Edit Mode,** the selection is done on mesh components:

- **Vertex Select:** Single points of a mesh are selected.
- **Edge Select:** Edges between two vertices are selected.
- **Face Select:** Select whole faces.

Switch between select modes using **1 (Vertex), 2 (Edge), and 3 (Face)** on the keyboard.

2. Nodes in Blender
Nodes are an essential part of Blender's shading, compositing, and geometry workflows. They provide the ability for non-destructive editing and for procedural workflows.

2.1 Understanding Nodes
A node contains a few elements:

- **Inputs:** Information that comes into the node.
- **Outputs:** Transformed information that leaves the node.
- **Properties:** Customizable options that alter node behavior.

Nodes are linked using **noodles (lines)** that create associations between them.

Organizing Nodes for Workflow Efficiency

In order to maintain node configurations tidy, Blender offers utilities like:

- **Sidebar & Node Groups:** Used in encapsulating multiple nodes into a single custom node.
- **Frame Nodes:** Helps in grouping complex node networks visually.
- **Reroute Nodes:** Makes reading possible by rerouting noodles.

3. Editing and Customizing Nodes
Node editing provides increased flexibility in shading, geometry, and compositing workflows.

- **Changing Node Properties:** Edit values such as colors, texture parameters, and blend modes.
- **Node Grouping:** Create reusable node groups for complex tasks.
- **Frame and Reroute Nodes:** Organize large node networks for readability.

Conclusion

Learning selection and node organization increases productivity in Blender. Whether it's selecting objects or organizing nodes effectively, these techniques guarantee a smoother workflow, making Blender an efficient tool for you as a creative professional, let's dive deeper!

Exploring Selections in Blender 4.4

Object, vertex, edge, and face selection is one of the most fundamental interactions within the 3D space in **Blender 4.4. Blender** assumes the **Left Mouse Button (LMB)** for selection by default, but other individuals may utilize **Right Mouse Button (RMB) selection** if they would rather have an alternate workflow within the **Preferences.**

To support different workflows, Blender has numerous selection tools accessible via many editors. Although the **default selection method remains unchanged,** the different key combinations in different editors to operate a selection task may be different. For instance, in many of the editors, adding to a selection is achieved with Shift + LMB, whereas in the **Outliner** it is achieved with **Ctrl + LMB.** Similarly, while most editors use **Ctrl + RMB** to perform **Lasso Selection,** node editors require **Ctrl + Alt + LMB** for the same task. Selection tools in Blender are usually found in **two modes:**

1. **Toolbar Selection Tools** – These are found in the **Toolbar** and are easier for users familiar with other software.
2. **Toolbar Selection Tools** – These tools are found in the **Select Menu** and they function slightly differently from their Toolbar counterparts.

Let us explore these tools in greater detail.

Toolbar Selection Tools

Selection tools in the **Toolbar** have an identical behavior when selecting individual objects—**clicking on an object selects it and deselects whatever selected objects might be present.** However, if you click while holding down **Shift**, you can **add an item to the selection** (if it isn't selected) or **remove it from the selection** (if it is selected).

The locations where these tools differ is with their **drag behavior.**

1. Tweak Selection Tool

- **Location:** `Toolbar → Tweak`
- **Shortcut:** `W`
- **Function:** Click and drag to move an item without explicitly selecting it first.
- This tool is useful for **quick adjustments** when working in **Edit Mode or Object Mode.**

2. Select Box Tool

- **Location:** `Toolbar → Select Box`
- **Shortcut:** `W`
- **Action:** Drag to create a rectangular selection box around items or objects.

  - Releasing the mouse **selects all items** enclosed in the box and unselects the rest.
  - Dragging while pressing **Shift adds** items to the selection.

- Dragging while pressing **Ctrl removes** the selected items.
- Dragging while holding **Spacebar** allows you to **move the selection box** interactively.

Example (Edit Mode):

1. Border Select Start
2.Selecting vertices
3. Selection complete

Select Box example (Edit Mode).

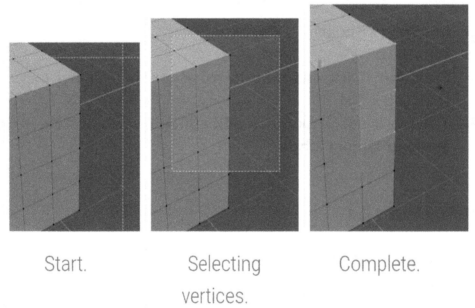

Start.   Selecting   Complete.

vertices.

3. Select Circle Tool

- **Location:** `Toolbar → Select Circle`
- **Shortcut:** `W`
- **Function:** Click and drag to create a **circular selection area.**

- Items inside the circle are selected, while those outside are deselected.
- Dragging while pressing **Shift** adds to the selection.
- Dragging while pressing **Ctrl** removes selected items.
- The **circle radius** can be set in **Tool Settings** (N Sidebar → Tool tab).

Object Mode Special Case:

As compared to **Select Box,** where an object is being selected as soon as any part of it comes within the selection box, **Select Circle** only selects an object if its **origin point** (orange dot) falls inside the circle. If the option **"Origins (All)"** under **Viewport Overlays** is enabled, these origins are visible for unselected objects.

Example (Edit Mode):

1.Circle Select Start
2.Selecting vertices
3. Selection complete

Select Circle example (Edit Mode).

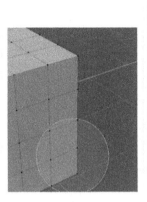 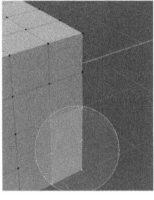 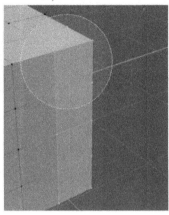

Start.   Selecting   Complete.
                vertices.

4. Select Lasso Tool

- **Location:** `Toolbar → Select Lasso`
- **Shortcut:** `W`
- **Function:** Click and drag to create a **freeform selection shape.**

- Releasing the mouse selects all items inside the lasso.
- Holding **Shift** while dragging **adds** to the selection.
- Holding **Ctrl** while dragging **removes** selected items.
- Holding down **Spacebar** and dragging allows you to **move the lasso shape** in a dynamic fashion.

Object Mode Special Case:

Just like **Select Circle, Lasso Select tool** in **Object Mode** only selects objects **if their origin points fall within the lasso shape.**

Example (Edit Mode):

1. Lasso Select Start
2. Selecting vertices
3. Selection complete

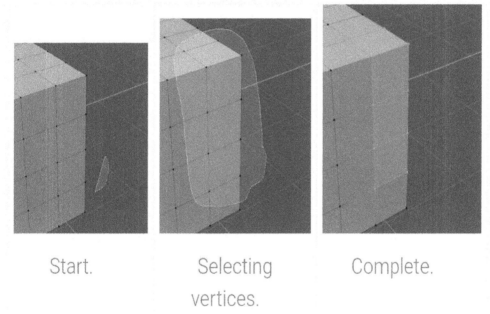

Select Lasso example (Edit Mode).

Start.   Selecting   Complete.
                vertices.

Selection Modes

All **selection tools** in the **Toolbar** have **five modes** that define how it will act on **current selections:**

Mode	Description
Set (Default)	Creates a **new selection**, overwriting the previous one.
Extend	Adds selected items to the **current selection.**
Subtract	Removes selected items from the **current selection.**
Invert (`Ctrl + I`)	**Reverses the selection—** deselected items get selected, and vice versa.
Intersect	Keeps only objects that intersect with the **current selection.**

Menu Selection Tools

While **Toolbar tools** are **activated when dragged, Menu selection tools** are **activated initially** before dragging the area for selection. The tools are slightly different in behavior.

1. Box Select (Menu Variant)

- **Where:** `Select → Box Select`
- **Shortcut:** `B`
- **Function:** Selects items inside a **dragged rectangular box.**

  - Unlike the **Toolbar version**, this tool **adds to the selection by default** (as opposed to replacing the selection).
  - Dragging with **Shift** removes items.
  - Dragging with the **Middle Mouse Button (MMB)** removes selected items.
  - Dragging while pressing **Spacebar** drags the box dynamically.

2. Circle Select (Menu Variant)

- **Where:** `Select → Circle Select`
- **Shortcut:** `C`
- **What:** Click and drag to **paint a selection** over objects.

  - The **circle size** can be changed using the **Mouse Wheel** or `Numpad + / -`.
  - This tool **remains active** until consciously shut down using `RMB`, `Return`, or `Esc`.
  - Holding **Shift** while dragging **removes items** from the selection.

3. Lasso Select (Menu Variant)

- **Location:** `Select → Lasso Select`
- **Shortcut:** `Ctrl + RMB`
- **Function:** Click and drag to **create a custom selection shape.**

  - Unlike **Toolbar Lasso**, this tool **adds to the selection by default.**
  - Pressing **Shift + Ctrl + RMB** removes objects.
  - Dragging while pressing **Spacebar** allows the **lasso shape to be moved dynamically.**

Mastering selection tools in Blender **enhances productivity in workflow**, especially when handling **complex 3D models**. Understanding **Toolbar vs. Menu selection tools,** selection modes, and **special cases** like origin-based selections in Object Mode allows it to be more accurately handled.

Now that you have heard about selection methods, you are ready to discover **advanced modeling workflows** in Blender 4.4!

Working with Nodes in Blender 4.4

Blender's **node-based system** is a very powerful system that's used for the purposes of shading, compositing, and geometry manipulation. Nodes make it possible for users to make complex effects and procedural workflows available using a visual programming interface. This chapter covers the **node editor interface, selection and arrangement methods, node editing, and professional-level organization tools** such as node groups, frames, and reroute nodes.

1. Introduction to Nodes

Nodes are individual processing units connected by "noodles" (lines) that pass data between one node and another. Nodes are used in **Shader Editor, Geometry Nodes, and Compositor** with a dynamic, non-destructive workflow.

2. Node Editor Interface

The **Node Editor** is the editor in which you create and edit nodes. It consists of:

- **Workspace:** The middle area where nodes reside.
- **Sidebar (N):** Shows other node properties.
- **Header Menu:** Holds options for adding, editing, and managing nodes.
- **Toolbar (T):** Offers tools for selection, transformation, and organization.

3. Navigating the Node Editor

Easy navigation is vital when dealing with intricate node configurations.

- **Pan:** MMB drag
- **Zoom**: Scroll wheel or Ctrl + MMB drag
- **Frame Selected:** Home or Numpad.
- **Fit View to All Nodes:** Shift + Home

4. Adding and Selecting Nodes
4.1 Adding Nodes

Nodes can be added using multiple methods:
- **Shift + A:** Opens the Add Node menu.
- **Drag & Drop:** From the sidebar or asset browser.

- **Search (F3):** Add a node to the graph and jump to the specified node.

4.2 Node Components

A node contains:
- **Title Bar:** The node name.
- **Sockets:** Connections points for entering and leaving values.
- **Properties Panel:** Editable node properties.

4.3 Node Selection

Selection behaves like object selection:
- **LMB:** Pick one node.
- **Shift + LMB:** Removers/adding from selection.
- **Box Select (B):** To select several nodes, drag it out.
- **Circle Select (C):** To pick out several nodes, paint it.
- **Lasso Select (Ctrl + RMB):** Draws freeform a selection zone.

5. Putting and Snapping Nodes
5.1 Rounding Nodes up for More Efficient Workflow
- **Moving Nodes:** (Grab) + Drag with G.
- **Align Nodes:** Right-click > Align Nodes.
- **Auto-Offset (Ctrl + Shift + RMB Drag):** Automatically adjusts connected nodes.
- **Snapping:** Enables precise alignment of nodes and connections.

6. Editing Nodes
6.1 Transforming Nodes
- **Move:** G
- **Scale:** S
- **Rotate:** R

6.2 Connecting and Disconnecting Sockets
- **Connect:** Drag from an output socket to an input socket.
- **Disconnect:** Drag a connection away or RMB > Disconnect Links.
- **Swap Connections:** Hold Shift while dragging a new connection over an existing one.

6.3 Copying and Duplicating Nodes
- **Copy (Ctrl + C) / Paste (Ctrl + V):** Copies selected nodes.
- **Duplicate (Shift + D):** Inserts a new standalone node.
- **Duplicate Linked (Alt + D):** Inserts a copy that gets properties from the original.

6.4 Deleting and Muting Nodes
- **Delete (X or Del):** Removes chosen nodes.
- **Mute (M):** Silences a node for a while without removing it.
- **Show/Hide (H):** Hides or displays a node.

6.5 Working with Layers
Some nodes provide support for layers in order to work with data flow. Use the **Layer Panel** to efficiently control them.

6.6 Connecting to Output
- Preview a node by pressing **Ctrl + Shift + LMB** within the viewport.
- Manually connect nodes to **Material Output** or **Composite Output** for outputting.

7. Sidebar & Node Groups
Sidebar Panels (N)
- **Node Panel:** Edit properties.

- **Tool Panel:** Gain access to selection and transformation tools.
- **View Panel:** Manage the look of the workspace.

7.2 Creating and Editing Node Groups

Grouping simplifies complicated configurations and enhances workflow efficiency.

- **Make Group (Ctrl + G):** Converts selected nodes into a single reusable group.
- **Insert Into Group:** Inserts a node into an existing group.
- **Edit Group (Tab):** Alters a group to modify it.
- **Ungroup (Ctrl + Alt + G):** Breaks a group down into separate nodes.
- **Reusing Node Groups:** Stored groups can be brought up in the **Add Menu** for reuse.

8. Advanced Node Organization
8.1 Frame Node

Frames structure and title node configurations.
- **Add Frame:** Select nodes > Right-click > Add Frame.
- **Resize Frame:** Drag the frame corners.
- **Label Frame:** Edit the title in the Sidebar.

8.2 Reroute Node

Reroute nodes make it easier to read by re-routing connections.
- **Add Reroute:** Drag from a socket and drop on an empty space.
- **Move Reroute**: G + Drag.
- **Delete Reroute:** X or Del.

Having the knowledge of how to correctly select, order, and handle nodes is crucial for an optimized workflow in Blender. When materials, compositing effects, or procedural geometry are being used, **readability and efficiency are increased through well-structured nodes.** With the help of selection tools, snapping settings, node groups, and reroute nodes, users can effortlessly build complex systems.

Working with Nodes

Blender has a number of node-based editors, each with a particular purpose. This is a general Blender tutorial on working with nodes, covering key concepts, interface, and basic tools. What comes next is an overview of the different kinds of nodes and their uses.

Example of a node editor.

Node Types in Blender

Icon	Name
	Geometry Nodes
	Shader Nodes
	Composite Nodes
	Texture Nodes

Node Type	Function
Geometry Nodes	Used for procedural modeling and object creation.
Shader Nodes	Utilized to create materials and define object surfaces.

Composite Nodes	Employed for post-processing and altering rendered images.
Texture Nodes	Designed to generate custom textures for materials.

Understanding the Node Editor Interface

Header Section

The **Header** at the top of the node editor contains menus, buttons, and options that differ based on the type of node tree being edited.

Menu Options

- **View** – Switches the editor's display settings on and off.
- **Select** – Provides tools for selecting individual or groups of nodes.
- **Add** – Provides an option to add new nodes to the editor.
- **Node** – Contains functions to edit selected nodes.
- **Use Nodes** – Enables or disables the node tree for rendering materials or compositing images.
- **Pin** – Causes the current material or texture to stay active in the editor even when other objects are selected.

- **Parent Node Tree** – Navigates to the parent node group when editing in nested node setups.
- **Snapping** – Aids in aligning and positioning nodes for a tidier appearance.
- **Overlays** – Presents supplementary visual details over the node tree, e.g., wire colors, context paths, and execution times.

Toolbar Section

The **Toolbar** offers instant access to common tools used to manipulate nodes.

Sidebar Section

The **Sidebar** displays properties for the current node along with other node editor settings.

Navigating the Node Editor

It is important to be able to navigate effectively when working with complex node setups. The following shortcuts allow users to move around the editor space:

- **Pan** – Middle Mouse Button (MMB) to pan the view.
- **Zoom** – Ctrl + MMB or mouse wheel to zoom in and out.
- **Frame Selected** – Numpad Period (.) to focus on selected nodes.
- **Frame All** – Home key to fit all nodes into view.

Adding and Managing Nodes

Inserting Nodes

Nodes can be added using:

- The **Add Menu** in the header.
- The **Shift + A** hotkey for direct access.
- Dragging a link from an input or output socket of a node already in the layout into an empty space, which calls up a search menu to insert a compatible node.

Once a new node has been inserted, it can be dragged and placed anywhere in the work area.

Understanding Node Parts in Blender 4.4

Blender node system comes with a consistent node structure for most node types. Each node contains significant parts such as the **title, sockets, inputs, outputs, and properties,** which define its function in a node-based workflow.

Title and Node Collapse

Each node has a title based on its name or type. The title is customizable by modifying the node's **Label** property by the users. A **collapse toggle** is offered at the left of the title bar, and through this, the users can collapse the display of the node. The same action can also be performed with the **H** shortcut.

When collapsed, a node displays only its essential components, keeping the workspace uncluttered.

How a node appears when collapsed.

Preview

There are a few nodes that offer **previews**, which place a small image over the node, displaying the node's output. Previews can be turned on and off with the **/ icons** at the top-right of the window. Users can also switch off previews for the whole node tree by altering the **Previews overlay toggle.**

Sockets

Sockets are input and output ports of nodes, shown as **small colored circles** on either side of a node. Users can hide unused sockets with **Ctrl + H.**

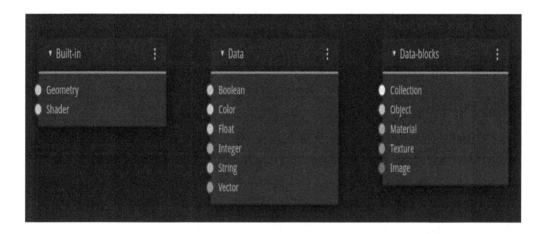

Sockets are color-coded to indicate the type of data they handle:

- **Shader (Bright Green)** – For shading in **Cycles** and **EEVEE.**
- **Geometry (Turquoise)** – For use in **Geometry Nodes.**
- **Boolean (Light Pink)** – For passing **true or false** values.
- **Color (Yellow)** – Processes color data, potentially with an alpha component.
- **Float (Gray)** – Processes single floating-point values or grayscale-based value maps.
- **Integer (Lime Green)** – Transfers whole numbers.
- **String (Light Blue)** – Passes text values.
- **Vector (Dark Blue)** – Represents coordinates or normal information.
- **Rotation (Pink)** – Stores rotation/quaternion values.
- **Matrix (Dark Pink)** – Processes **4×4 transformation matrices.**

There are sockets that are specifically meant to process **data-blocks**, such as:

- **Collection (White)** – Downloads a collection data-block.
- **Object (Orange)** – Downloads an object data-block.
- **Material (Salmon)** – Downloads a material data-block.
- **Texture (Pink)** – Downloads a texture data-block.
- **Image (Apricot)** – Downloads an image data-block.

Inputs and Outputs

- **Inputs** are located on the **left side** of the node and supply the data needed for its operation. If not connected, most inputs have a **default value,** which can be controlled by numeric, color, or vector controls.
- **Outputs** are located on the **right side** and are used to connect nodes together in the workflow.

Some nodes have **multi-input sockets**, which are shaped like an **ellipsis** instead of a circle, to indicate that they can accept more than one connection.

Socket Conversion

Blender accepts certain socket types to be **converted** either **implicitly** (automatically) or **explicitly** (using conversion nodes).

Implicit Conversions

These are done automatically when connecting sockets of another type:

- **Color** ↔ **Vector** – Connects color channels to vector components.
- **Color** ↔ **Float** – Connects colors to grayscale.
- **Float** ↔ **Vector** – A float value sets the identical value on every vector component.
- **Float** ↔ **Boolean** – Positive floats are mapped to true, and true is mapped to

1, **false** to 0.
- **Float** ↔ **Integer** – Floats are directly converted from integers; floats are truncated upon being converted into integers.
- **Rotations** ↔ **Matrices** – Mapped rotation values into transformation matrices.

Explicit Conversions

For more precise control of the conversion, some conversions must employ specific nodes such as:
- **Shader To RGB Node**
- **RGB To BW Node**
- **Math Node** (with built-in functions for degree/radian conversion).

Node Properties

The majority of nodes possess **user-configurable properties** which decide their input processing and output creation. They are shown **between the input and output regions.**

For example, the **Chroma Key node** has several controls that are adjustable and affect how it isolates colors in an image.

By understanding these fundamental elements, users can effectively create and edit node-based workflows in Blender and enhance their 3D modeling, shading, compositing, and animation work.

CHAPTER 14:

NODE SELECTION AND ORGANIZATION IN BLENDER 4.4

Blender has a number of tools for multiple selection and organization to enhance node handling for efficiency and neatness. It is necessary to understand these features to optimize procedures, whether it is editing shaders, compositing, or working with geometry nodes.

Node Selection

Efficient node selection is crucial when editing and working with complex node hierarchies. Blender offers a number of selection options:

Simple Selection Operations
- **Select All** – `A`
- Chooses all nodes within the editor.
- **Deselect All** – `Alt + A`
- Removes selection from all the selected nodes.
- **Invert Selection** – `Ctrl + I`
- Toggles the current selection, tagging unselected nodes and unselecting selected nodes.

Selection Tools

- **Box Select** – `B`: Allows the users to make a box over nodes in an effort to select multiple of them.
- **Circle Select:** Allows selection by coloring over nodes with a round brush.
- **Lasso Select:** Makes selections of nodes by creating a freeform selection shape.

Selection Based on Node Connections

- **Select Linked From** – `L`

Extends selection to cover all nodes **connected to the inputs** of the selected node(s).

- **Select Linked To** – `Shift + L`

Expands selection to all nodes **attached to the outputs** of the active node(s).

Selecting Similar Nodes

- **Select Grouped** – `Shift + G`

Selects nodes with properties similar to the active node, such as:

- **Type** – Selects all nodes of the same type (e.g., all **Math** nodes).
- **Color** – Selects nodes of the same **type custom color** (configured in the Sidebar).
- **Prefix/Suffix** – Compares nodes by the start or end of their name.

Quick Node Navigation

- **Activate Same Type (Previous/Next)** – `Shift + ] / Shift + [`

- Highlights the previous or next node of the same type, activates it, and shows it.
- **Find Node** – `Ctrl + F`
- Pops open a **search pop-up** to search for a node by name.

Multiple Selection

- **Select Multiple Nodes** – `Shift + Left Mouse Button (LMB)`

Turns adding/removing nodes to/from the selection on and off.

Arranging Nodes

Node layouts should be kept tidy in order to maintain them as readable and efficient as possible.

Snapping

Nodes can be snapped and arranged to a grid for tidiness.

- Toggle snapping on and off by clicking the **snap icon (/)** in the top of the editor.
- Temporarily enable snapping while dragging nodes with **Ctrl.**

Auto-Offset

Auto-offset moves currently placed nodes automatically when a new node is dropped between them, keeping the layout tidy.

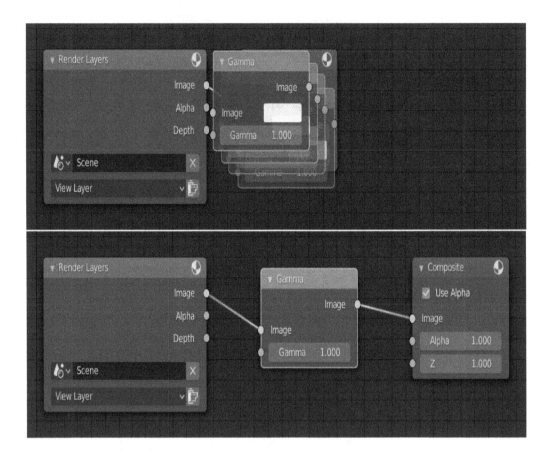

How Auto-Offset Works

1. When dropping a node **with one or more input and one or more output sockets** onto a connection, Auto-Offset **moves adjacent nodes** out of the way.
2. **Offset direction** is determined by the setup and can be changed with T while sliding the node.

Adjusting Auto-Offset

- **Turn Auto-Offset on/off** under **Preferences**.
- **Auto-Offset Margin** can be tweaked under the **Editing options** within Preferences.

With this selection and arranging functions, people are able to quickly arrange nodes, increase workflow speed, and maintain a clean workspace within Blender's node editors.

Editing Nodes in Blender 4.4

During the editing of nodes in Blender, you need to edit them as efficiently as possible to have smooth workflows. This section discusses how to move, rotate, resize, join, and sever nodes so that your workflow is smoother.

Moving, Rotating, and Resizing Nodes

Moving Nodes

To move a node, you can either:
- Click and drag across any part of an otherwise empty space on the node.
- Press **G,** move the mouse, and left-click (LMB) to confirm the new position.

Also, when you drag a node over an existing connection, Blender will position the node along the path of the connection. It does so by automatically linking the node with the best matching input and output sockets. In case you want to prevent Blender from automatically linking, keep **Alt** down while dragging the node.

For an organized and neat layout, it is recommended that your nodes have an orderly flow—from left to right and from top to bottom. This makes it easier to trace data processing via the node system.

Resizing Nodes

To adjust the width of a node, simply drag the left or right edge. It is useful when you need extra room to view the contents of the node or like your work area to be uncluttered.

Rotating and Scaling Nodes

Rotation **(R)** and scaling **(S)** are only available when more than one node is chosen. These operations change the relative positions of the nodes but not their internal characteristics.

Connecting and Disconnecting Sockets

Connecting Nodes

To create a connection between nodes:
1. Click (LMB) on an output socket and drag a link from it.
2. Drag the link to an input socket on another node.
3. Release the LMB to complete the connection.
A single output socket can be linked to numerous input sockets, but a single input socket will typically only accept a single connection unless it is a multi-socket input (which is displayed as a pill-shaped socket).

Advanced Link Manipulation

- **Interchanging Multiple Links:** Click and hold **Alt** when dragging a link to interchange multiple links of the same category.
- **Moving Outgoing Links:** To move an outgoing link instead of adding a new link, hold **Ctrl** and drag from an output socket.

Also, if you have a node with no connection, you can **drag it over an existing link** and release when the link is highlighted. Blender will automatically insert it into the chain.

Connecting Many Nodes Automatically

If you have multiple nodes to join:
- Select them and press **F** to automatically join open sockets.
- Press **Shift + F** to replace any links that may already be there with new ones.

Disconnecting Nodes

Manually Removing Connections
- Click and **drag a link away** from an input socket to break the connection.
- This makes the socket free for new connections.

Cutting Multiple Links
- Press **Ctrl + RMB,** and draw a line across one or more links to cut them.
- Keep in mind that this shortcut usually opens **Lasso Select,** but in node editors, **Ctrl + Alt + LMB** is used for lasso selection instead.

Completely Detaching Links
- **Alt + LMB drag** allows you to cut all links that are related to an elected node and relocate it somewhere else.

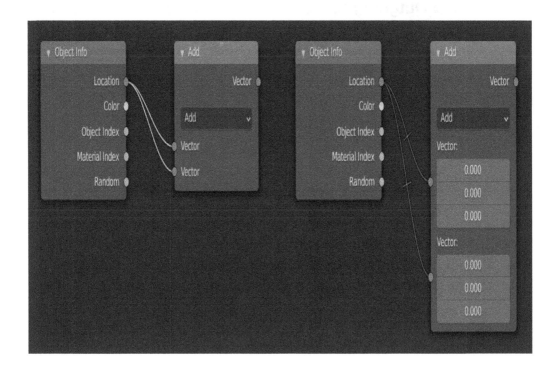

Copying, Pasting, and Duplication of Nodes

Copies & Pasting Nodes
- **Ctrl + C** to copy selected nodes.
- **Ctrl + V** to paste them in the same place they were copied from.

When duplicating, keep in mind that nodes appear in the very same location they were copied from, and you may have to drag them by hand.

Duplicating Nodes

- **Shift + D** to duplicate an individual or group of nodes.
- After duplicated, drag duplicate node(s) and click **LMB** or press **Enter** to confirm.

⚠ **Warning:** Unless you move a copied node, it will exactly sit on top of the original, and thus you won't be able to see it. If in doubt, try nudging the node a bit to check if there are any hidden duplicates.

Duplicating with Shared Data

- **Alt + D** copies a node but does not make its data unshared.
- It does imply that variations to one node take effect throughout its copies, helping maintain constant configurations in all the nodes.

Removing and Muting Nodes

Removing Nodes
- **X or Delete** keys press to delete nodes which are currently highlighted.
- **Ctrl + X** removes nodes with reconnections made from and to them for maintaining flow continuity.

Muting Nodes
- **Press M** to silence a node so that data passes through it without affecting the output.
- Muted nodes are represented by red links.

Tip: An individual node link can be silenced using the **Mute Links** feature **(Ctrl + Alt + RMB).**

Hiding and Showing Node Elements

Collapsing Nodes
- Press H to hide a node such that only the header of the node is displayed.
- Or, you can toggle it by clicking on the tiny triangle within the node header.

Previewing Node Effects

- **Shift + H** turns node preview on and off, showing a small preview of the effect applied by that node.

Hiding Unused Sockets
- **Ctrl + H** conceals all sockets that are not attached to another node.

Concealing All Node Properties
- Use **Toggle Node Options** to show or conceal all properties that can be modified within a node.

Manipulating Render Layers in Nodes

Reading Render Layers

- **Ctrl + R** reloads all render layers from the cache.
- This serves to minimize RAM usage during rendering and makes it possible to recover data from a failed render.

⚠ **Note**: This feature is supported only in the **Compositor** node editor.

Linking to the Final Output

- **Shift + Alt + LMB** automatically connects a node's output to the final output of the node tree.
- It works in various node editors:
  - **Compositor:** It links to the Composite node.
  - **Shader Editor:** It links to the Material Output or World Output node.
  - **Geometry Nodes:** It links to the Group Output node.

Using these techniques, you can efficiently manage your node setups in Blender such that they are readable and convenient to use.

Understanding the Sidebar in Blender's Node Editor

The **Sidebar** in Blender's Node Editor provides essential controls for managing nodes, customizing their appearance, and accessing various tools. It contains multiple tabs, each serving a specific purpose to help streamline your workflow. Below is a breakdown of the key sections within the Sidebar.

The Node Panel

This panel provides controls related to the selected node.

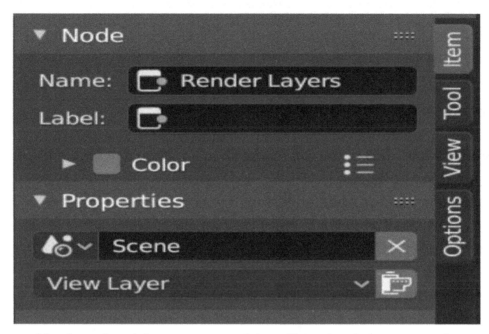

Node tab with a compositing Render Layers node selected.

Node Name

Each node of a node tree possesses an identification name. Even though the name is automatically provided, it exists to distinguish between nodes, especially when there is a huge network of nodes involved.

Label

Unique labels for nodes can be introduced by modifying the text field. This makes the identification and arranging of nodes by sight even simpler.

Warning Propagation

This is specific to **Geometry Nodes** and determines which of the node's warnings will be passed on to the parent **Node Group** or **Modifier**.

Color Customization

The background color of a node is normally governed by Blender's theme. You can override this, however, and set a custom color for improved readability. This proves useful in intricate node graphs, where you can visually differentiate between nodes.

- **Color Picker:** Enables you to pick a node color of your choice.
- **Save as Preset:** You can save frequently used colors as presets so that it is easier to maintain consistency for multiple projects.

Node Color Specials

This menu contains special operations for dealing with custom node colors.

- **Copy Color:** Allows you to copy the color of the currently highlighted node and apply it to all the nodes you have highlighted, giving a uniform look throughout your process.

Properties Panel

Properties here are node-dependent on the selected node. For instance:
- A **Mix Node** would have blending properties.
- A **Mask Node** would have alternative controls relevant to masking operations.

The section dynamically updates in accordance with the currently active tool. It provides one with quick access to settings and options relevant to the selected tool.

Active Tool
- Displays tool options relevant to the active tool.
- It affects directly how the tool behaves with nodes.

3. View Panel
This panel controls the **visual settings** of the Node Editor.

Annotations
- You may use the **Annotate Tool** (in the Toolbar) to add freehand notes or highlight specific parts in the Node Editor.
- This is convenient for leaving reminders, marking important node groups, or collaborating with others.

The **Sidebar** is an integral component of Blender's Node Editor, keeping you organized, enabling you to customize your workspace, and swiftly managing nodes. Through **Compositing, Shading, to Geometry Nodes**, these tools optimize control and improve workflow.

Understanding Node Groups in Blender 4.4

Node Groups in Blender are a strong feature for managing complicated node arrangements, enhancing workflow productivity, and facilitating reuse in other projects. Consider them as **functions in**

programming—you can wrap a group of nodes into a single entity and utilize it several times, even in various node trees.

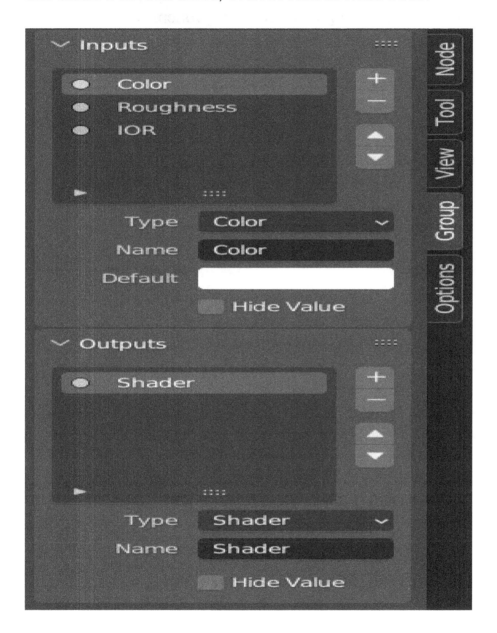

As an example, when you have a **"Wood" material** and wish to change its color without copying the whole node configuration, a Node Group enables you to keep the basic wood texture centralized while you change only the color. By doing so, any subsequent adjustments (like grain density) would only have to be done once within the Node Group, making it a time and effort-saving approach.

Key Features of Node Groups

- Encapsulation & Reusability
- A Node Group is a solitary node that contains multiple nodes.
- It can be reused in other node trees without duplication.
- Can be customized using input parameters.

Nesting Support
- Node Groups can contain other Node Groups.
- However, **recursive node groups** (a group that includes itself) are not allowed to prevent infinite loops.

Hidden Node Groups
- Like other Blender data-blocks, node groups whose names start with \"\\\" are hidden from menus and can only be opened by searching.
- This is helpful for **node asset authors** to prevent internal sub-groups from being visible to end users.

Creating & Using Node Groups

Grouping Nodes
To make a Node Group:

1. **Select the nodes** that you wish to include.
2. **Press `Ctrl+G`** or go to **Node → Make Group.**

3. The chosen nodes will now be inside a **new Node Group,** which is indicated by a **green title bar.**

4. The new Node Group will be named **"NodeGroup",** **"NodeGroup.001"**, etc. You can rename it for clarity.

Tip: When appending Node Groups between blend files, Blender does not differentiate between **Material** and **Composite Node Groups.** It's a good practice to have a consistent naming convention to distinguish them.

Handling Inputs & Outputs

A **Group Input** and **Group Output** node are automatically generated when a Node Group is created:

- **Group Input:** Handles incoming connections to the node group.
- **Group Output:** Outputs processed data from the node group.

Including Custom Inputs & Outputs
To input an additional parameter into the group:
- **Drag a link** from the **empty socket** on the right of **Group Input** to the target node.

Same for outputs:
- Link a node's output to the **Group Output** node.

Node Group Properties

Group Panel (Sidebar → Group)

Settings pertaining to the node group's identity and looks are in this panel.

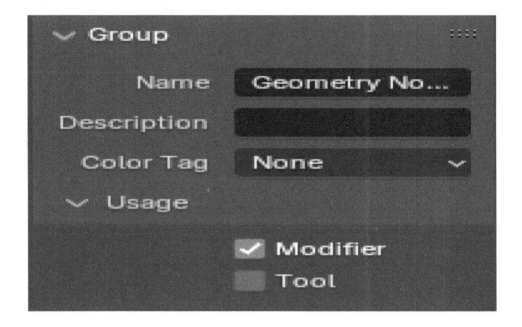

- **Name** – Display name of the Node Group.
- **Description** – Tooltip text displayed on hover over the node.
- **Color Tag** – Alters the color of the header of the node for easier organization.
- **Node Width** – Specifies the width of new group nodes created.

Note: You can set the default width based on the **parent node** in the current context.

Usage in Geometry Nodes

If a Node Group is created in the **Geometry Node Editor,** there are a few additional options:

- **Modifier:** The group is designed to be used with the **Geometry Nodes Modifier.**
- **Tool:** The group is meant to be utilized as a tool within Blender's node system.

Tip: With both "Usage" options disabled, the node group won't appear in the **data-block menu.** To restore it, insert the group into another node group and enter Edit Mode (`Tab`) to re-enable one of the usages.

Working with Group Sockets

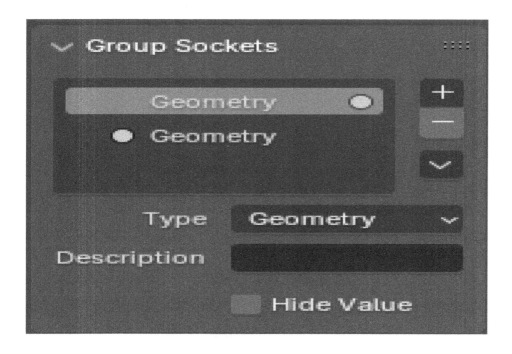

The **Group Sockets Panel** (Sidebar → Group → Group Sockets) allows you to:

- **Add, remove, and reorder inputs/outputs** for better organization.

- **Edit socket names** for clarity in the node interface.
- **Set default values** for unconnected inputs.

Advanced Options
- **Min & Max Values:** Define UI limits (but do not restrict actual data).
- **Hide Value:** Prevents an input from being displayed in the node UI.
- **Single Value Mode:** Restricts inputs to single values instead of **Fields**.

Tip: You can create **nested panels** for organizing inputs more effectively. Dragging one panel onto another in the UI list will nest them.

Key Differences: Node Group Output vs. Other Output Nodes

All Node Editors in Blender have an "**Output**" section in the **Add menu,** with nodes like:
- Material Output
- Composite Output

These should **not** be confused with the **Group Output** node, which is for use within **Node Groups.** The **Group Output** node will only function inside a Node Group and is used to define outputs for a group.

Node Groups are the secret to **workflow optimization, reduction of complexity**, and **improved reusability** in Blender. By having control over them, you'll be capable of creating more efficient and organized node trees for **shading, compositing, and geometry nodes.**

Node Group Advanced Management in Blender 4.4

Node management within the **Node Editor** is one of the most crucial methods of workflow optimization and project organization within Blender. One of the highly effective methods of doing so is by using **Node Groups,** which enable wrapping a group of nodes within a single wrapper. Not only is it utilized for maintaining complex node trees organized, but also for reusability, modularity, and simpler changes.

This section gives a **step-by-step breakdown** of managing Node Groups, from adding nodes to an existing group, modifying groups, ungrouping, and recycling node groups in various projects.

Inserting Nodes Into an Existing Group

What Does This Do?
The **Insert Into Group** tool lets you transfer chosen nodes into a pre-existing **Node Group** without disrupting their connections. It is convenient when you need to **refine or expand a Node Group** without destroying the logic of the node tree already in place.

How to Use:
1. **Select Nodes** – Pick the nodes that you wish to transfer **into** a group that already exists.
2. **Select the Destination Group** – Ensure that the last node that is chosen is the **destination Node Group.**

3. **Execute the Command –**
  - Go to **Node → Insert Into Group** in the menu.
  - The nodes that were chosen will now be inserted into the chosen Node Group.

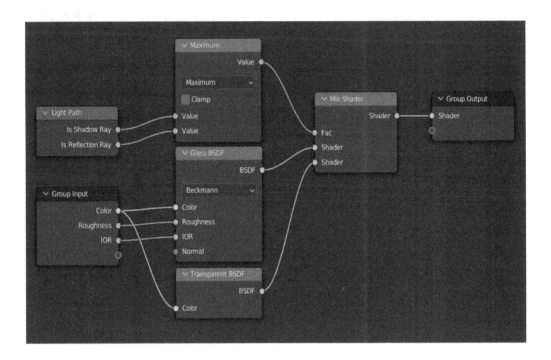

Blender's Treatment of Inserted Nodes

  - The nodes to be moved are **clustered within the Node Group** so that they retain their connection logic.
  - A **new Group Input and Group Output node** can be added to incorporate these nodes within the group framework.
  - In case any new input/output sockets are added, the **existing inputs/outputs of the Group will be modified** to include them.

Important Rules:
  - A Node Group **can have only one Group Input and one Group Output** node.

- If there are more than one input/output nodes, Blender will ask you to **merge them manually.**

Editing a Node Group

Going In and Out of a Node Group
After creating a Node Group, you can edit its content by going inside its inner node tree.

Enter the Group:
- Choose the Node Group and hit **Tab** or use **Node → Edit Group.**

- Exit the Group:
- Hit **Tab** again (or use **Ctrl + Tab)** to go back to the parent node tree.

Breadcrumb Navigation:
- The top-left corner of the Node Editor shows the group hierarchy, so you know where you are within the node structure.

Changing Group Inputs and Outputs

Within a Node Group, Group Input and Group Output nodes manage data flow.

- **Adding an Input:** Drag a connection from the **Group Input** node to any socket in the internal nodes..
- Adding an Output: Connect a node's output to an empty socket on the **Group Output** node..
- Rearranging Inputs/Outputs: In the **Group Sockets Panel,** you can rename, reorder or remove input/output sockets to make it more organized.

Tip: When editing complex Node Groups, use **frame nodes** (Shift + A → Layout → Frame) to visually organize sections inside the group.

Ungrouping Nodes

What Happens When You Ungroup?
The **Ungroup** operation breaks apart a Node Group and restores its individual nodes into the workspace.

- **All internal connections remain intact,** ensuring that the workflow remains functional.
- **No data is lost,** and you are able to edit or reconnect the individual nodes later on.

How to Ungroup a Node Group

1. **Select the Node Group** – Click on the group in the Node Editor.
2. **Ungroup the Nodes:**
   - Press **Ctrl + Alt + G.**
   - Or go to **Node → Ungroup** in the menu.

Separating, Copying, and Moving Nodes

At times, you may wish to extract only specific portions of a Node Group instead of ungrouping the whole thing.

- **Separate P** – Enables you to delete only the chosen nodes from a Node Group and leave the rest of it intact.

- **Copy to Parent Node Tree** – Duplicates the selected nodes into the parent workspace **without removing them from the group**.
- **Move to Parent Node Tree** – Moves the selected nodes **out of the Node Group,** completely removing them from the group structure.

Reusing Node Groups Across Projects

- **Adding Existing Node Groups in the Same Project**

Once a Node Group is created, it can be reused in the current project:

1. **Shortcut:** Press **Shift + A** → Go to **Add** → **Group** and select the saved Node Group.
2. **Modify as Needed:** Each instance of the group remains linked, so editing one **affects all instances** unless you create a separate copy.

Importing Node Groups from Other Blender Files

To reuse Node Groups from other. blend files, use **Link/Append:**
1. **Go to** `File → Link/Append`.
2. **Select the. blend file** containing the Node Group.
3. **Navigate to** `Node Tree → [Your Node Group Name]`.
4. **Click Append or Link** to add the Node Group to your project.

 Linking vs. Appending:
- **Linking** keeps the Node Group referenced from the original file (any updates in the source file will affect the linked version).
- **Appending** makes an independent copy of the Node Group in the new file.

Best Practices for Node Groups

✓ **Use Descriptive Names** – Instead of generic names like **NodeGroup.001**, use clear, meaningful names like **GlassShaderGroup** or **DustEffectGroup**.

✓ **Organize Inputs Logically** – Place frequently adjusted inputs at the top to make them easier to access.

✓ **Color Code Node Groups** – Assign colors to differentiate **material**, **compositing**, and **geometry** Node Groups.

✓ **Minimize Excessive Inputs** – Keep input sockets **minimal and relevant** to avoid cluttering the node interface.

✓ **Modular Design** – Design Node Groups as a **standalone, reusable unit** and not as dependent on external nodes.

✓ **Performance Optimization** – Avoid **unnecessary calculations** in Node Groups; every calculation can push up render times.

Node Groups is one of Blender's most powerful tool features for the management of complex node setups in an efficient manner. Understanding how to insert, edit, ungroup, and reuse Node Groups helps to streamline your workflow when implementing modular setups that enhance reusability across different projects. By following best practices regarding clarity, organization, and efficiency in node-based workflows, you can work with shaders, compositing, or procedural geometry.

Frame and Reroute Nodes in Blender 4.4:

Tidy Your Node Workflow into Shape

With more node configurations in Blender coming more and more complex, clean and tidy it must be. While **Node Groups** is a great way to bundle away reusable functions, sometimes you just need ways to **clean up** your node tree without necessarily changing the order. This is where **Frame Nodes** and **Reroute Nodes** come into the equation.

- **Frame Nodes** assist in keeping similar nodes in order by enclosing them in a visual container.
- **Reroute Nodes** enable tidier, more organized node arrangements by routing connections without redundant overlaps.

Both tools greatly enhance workflow readability and efficiency without changing functionality.

Frame Nodes: Organizing Your Node Tree

What Is a Frame Node?
A **Frame Node** is a simple container that keeps similar nodes grouped together in an organized manner. Frames do not alter the behavior of the nodes contained within them, unlike Node Groups.

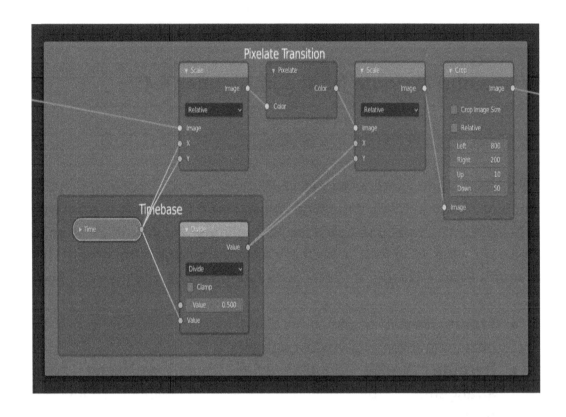

When to Use Frame Nodes?

- When your node layout becomes too large and cluttered.
- When you need **better visual organization** without concealing logic in a Node Group.
- When you want to clearly separate different parts of your node tree, such as **Base Color, Detail Mapping,** or **Final Effects** in a shader.

How to Use Frame Nodes

Creating a Frame Node

1. **Shortcut:** Press **Ctrl + J** following the selection of multiple nodes so that they automatically get wrapped into a new Frame.
2. **Manual Method:**
   - Press **Shift + A** → Navigate to **Layout** → Select **Frame.**
   - **Move and resize** the Frame by hand to enclose the affected nodes.

Editing Frame Nodes

Changing Frame Properties

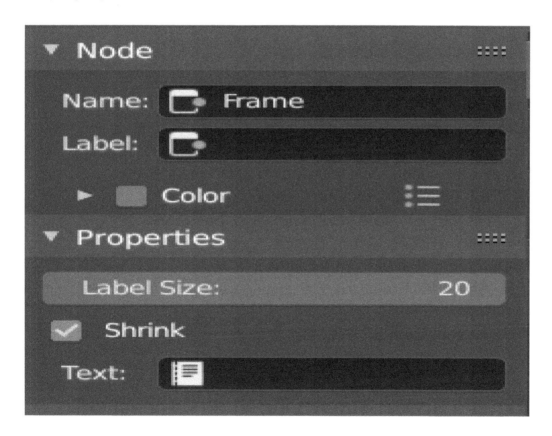

Once a Frame Node is created, you can adjust its appearance and behavior:

- **Label Size** – Scales the title font of the frame. You can use smaller labels for lower-level frames.
- **Shrink Frame** – Automatically resizes the Frame size to fit its contents, eliminating unnecessary space.
- **Enabled:** The Frame automatically resizes whenever nodes inside are rearranged.
- **Disabled:** The Frame is resizable manually.
- **Text Display** – Allows the Frame to display read-only text from a **Text Data-Block** (prepared using the Text Editor). It is handy for **inserting descriptions** or instructions into the node editor.

Handling Nodes inside a Frame

Inserting Nodes in a Frame
- **Drag and Drop** – Simply drag a node into the Frame.
- **Parenting Shortcut:**
1. Select the node(s) that you want to add.
 2. Press **Shift** and select the Frame.
 3. Press **Ctrl + P** to parent the nodes to the Frame.

Unparenting Nodes from a Frame
- **Shortcut:** Press **Alt + P** to unparent selected nodes from a Frame.
- **Manual Method:** Drag and drop the node past the Frame.

Reroute Nodes: Simplifying Node Connections

What Is a Reroute Node?

A **Reroute Node** is similar to a connection junction point for nodes. It allows you to remove cluttered and overlapping node links by rerouting them onto neater, more organized paths.

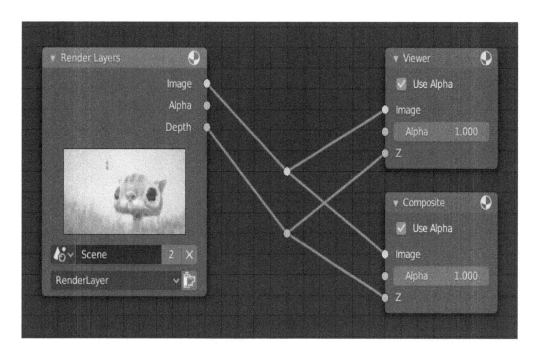

When to Use Reroute Nodes?

- When you need to **eliminate connection clutter** in dense node trees.
- When multiple nodes receive the same input but direct connections produce **cluttered overlapping lines.**
- When you want to create **logical routes** for better readability of your node setup.

How to Add a Reroute Node

Quick Method (Auto-Insert a Reroute Node)

1. **Hold Shift + Right Mouse Button (RMB)** while sweeping across an existing connection.
2. A Reroute Node will be automatically inserted at the point where your cursor crosses the link.

Manual Method

1. Press **Shift + A** → Go to **Layout** → Select **Reroute**.
2. Place the Reroute Node in the desired position.
3. Manually connect it between nodes.

Reroute Nodes Editing

- **Input Sockets:** A Reroute Node **accepts only one input.**
- **Output Sockets:** It has **many output connections,** so it's ideal to disseminate a single value to other nodes.
- **Repositioning:** Simply drag a Reroute Node to resort node connections without interfering with links.

Tip: To remove a Reroute Node without severing the link between the nodes, select it and click **X.** The links will fill in the gap for you.

Best Practices for Using Frame and Reroute Nodes

✓ **Use Frame Nodes to Organize Different Parts of a Node Tree** – Label frames clearly to read them easily (e.g., "Texture Control," "Lighting Adjustments").

✓ **Alternate Frames and Reroutes for Clarity** – Frames facilitate visual grouping of nodes, and Reroutes provide uncluttered connections.

✓ **Color Code Key Frames** – Color different Frames to group nodes further.

✓ **Use Few Reroute Nodes** – Use them to organize node connections but avoid using too many so as not to add unnecessary complexity.

✓ **Label Complex Reroutes** – If a Reroute Node is utilized in a crucial section of your setup, label it with the Node Properties panel for clarity.

Within Blender's **Node Editor,** having your node setups **organized, readable, and efficient** is critical for productivity. **Frame Nodes** and **Reroute Nodes** offer straightforward yet effective means to do this:

- **Frame Nodes** organize similar nodes into groups for **improved organization and readability.**
- **Reroute Nodes** simplify node connections, eliminating clutter and enhancing **visual flow.**

By using these tools efficiently, you can **improve your workflow**, making your **shaders, compositing setups, and geometry nodes more organized and easier to manage.**

CHAPTER 15

COLLABORATING WITH EDITORS IN BLENDER 4.4:

Blender provides a vast array of **Editors** to accomplish specific tasks, no matter if you are modeling within **3D, animating, texturing, scripting, or data handling.** The editors allow one to **look at, change, and administer** different types of data in a Blender project.

Each **Editor** is contained within an **Area**, which determines its size as well as where it will appear in the **Blender interface.** A **single workspace** can contain more than a single editor, and the same kind of editor can be used repeatedly in distinct areas simultaneously for even greater workflow efficiency.

How to Access and Switch Editors

In order to switch the **Editor type** for an area:
1. Press the **Editor Type Selector** (leftmost button in an editor's title bar).
2. Choose from the supported **Editor types** in the drop-down menu.

This feature allows users to **tweak their working area,** and to have several windows open of a particular editor, if necessary.

Editor types of Blender

Blender's Editors can be classified according to the function they serve:

1. **General Editors** – For use in modeling, shading, texturing, and compositing.
2. **Animation Editors** – For use in keyframing, timeline control, and motion curves.
3. **Scripting Editors** – For use in writing and running Python scripts in Blender.
4. **Data Editors** – For use in controlling objects, materials, files, and properties.
5. **Preferences** – For use in setting up Blender's behavior and interface.

General Editors

These editors are used for **3D modeling, texture mapping, compositing, shading, and video editing.**

➤ **3D Viewport**
- The **primary workspace** where the 3D models are created, edited, and rendered.
- Offers different views: **solid, wireframe, material preview, and rendered mode.**
- Is used for modeling, sculpting, animating, and object transformations.

➤ Image Editor

- Edits and renders **image textures, renders, and baked images.**
- Offers color correction, masking, and overpainting support over textures.

➤ UV Editor

- Used for **UV mapping,** where the textures were properly mapped on 3D models.
- Allows precise realignment of **UV islands, seams, and stretching.**

➤ Compositor

- Blender's **node-based compositing** compositing tool for layering **post-processing effects** over renders.
- Utilized for **color grading, green screen effects, and visualization additions.**

➤ Texture Nodes

- Encompasses the creation of **procedural textures** through a node-based approach.

➤ Geometry Node Editor

- Utilized for **procedural modeling and object editing** through node-based processes.
- Facilitates **parametric modeling** and high-end object manipulation.

➤ Shader Editor

- Enables the creation and editing of **materials** through **node-based shading workflows.**

- Utilized to model intricate **PBR materials, procedural shaders, and bespoke effects.**

➤ **Video Sequencer**
  - A **non-linear video editor** within Blender.
  - Incorporates **cutting, layering, transitions, and audio editing.**

➤ **Movie Clip Editor**
  - Utilized for **motion tracking, rotoscoping, and stabilizing footage** in Blender.
  - Essential for **visual effects (VFX) and integrating 3D elements into live-action video.**

Animation Editors

These editors help control animations, keyframes, and motion curves.

➤ **Dope Sheet**
  - A **timeline-based** editor for managing animation keyframes.
  - Allows for **grouping, re-timing, and editing animations more efficiently.**

➤ **Timeline**
  - Displays **keyframes and playback controls** for animations.
  - Used for **run-time playback and fundamental animation sequencing.**

➤ **Graph Editor**
  - Provides a **graphical view** of editing **motion curves and interpolation.**

- Extremely crucial for **smooth motion transition creation and animation fine-tuning.**

➤ **Drivers Editor**
- Can be employed to create **custom dependencies** among objects, properties, and animations.
- Employed to **automate** animation behaviors.

➤ **Nonlinear Animation (NLA Editor)**
- Enables **layered animation control** and the blending of animation sequences.
- Used for **creating complex animations, looping motions, and action blending**.

Scripting Editors

For users who want to **extend Blender's functionality with Python scripting.**

➤ **Text Editor**
- A built-in **code editor** used for writing and executing **Python scripts.**
- Can be used for **defining tools, automating scripts, and executing scripts within Blender.**

➤ **Python Console**
- A **console mode Python command interface** within Blender.
- Can be employed for **scripting, testing, and debugging Python commands.**

➤ **Info Editor**

- Shows a **history of the commands** which have been run in Blender.
- Convenient to **log actions of the scripts and debug the scripts.**

Data Editors

Editors help with the handling of objects, materials, and scene attributes.

➤ Outliner
- Displays a **hierarchical structure** of every object within the scene.
- Allows users to **hide, lock, rename, or group** objects quickly.

➤ Properties Editor
- **Destination point** for changing object settings, materials, rendering options, and physics simulations.
- Organized into several tabs for **easy access to various settings.**

➤ File Browser
- For importing, exporting, and organizing external assets.
- Enables users to browse **Blender files (.blend), images, and external libraries.**

➤ Asset Browser
- A special area for **organizing reusable assets,** such as **materials, models, and brushes.**
- Enables simple **drag-and-drop** integration of saved assets.

➤ **Spreadsheet Editor**
- Displays **scene data, attributes, and geometry details** in a table.
- Frequently used in combination with **Geometry Nodes** to inspect and modify data values.

Preferences Editor

➤ **Blender Preferences**
- The central control panel for **tuning Blender's behavior and interface.**
- Allows setting of **keymaps, themes, add-ons, input devices, and system settings.**

Best Practices to Use Blender Editors in the Most Efficient Way

✓ **Customize Your Layout** – Layout editors based on your workflow (for example, a 3D Viewport + Shader Editor + Properties to accomplish shading work).

✓ **Use Multiple Editor Instances** – Keep the same editor open in more than one location to edit multiple parts simultaneously.

✓ **Save Custom Workspaces** – You can save your preferred editor layouts as custom workspaces for quick recall.

✓ **Learn Keyboard Shortcuts** – Blender offers enormous shortcuts for switching editors and navigating, making it faster and more efficient.

Blender's **Editor system** is a very flexible and powerful means of creating **3D modeling, texturing, animation, compositing, scripting, and asset management.** Whether you are **modeling a character, modeling materials, creating procedural effects, or animating keyframes,** there is a specific editor that suits your particular demands such that any aspect of your project can be carefully controlled and adjusted.

By studying **Blender's Editors,** you'll be able to **optimize your workflow,** boost **productivity,** and **access the full potential** of Blender 4.4.

Exploring The 3D Viewport in Blender 4.4:

The **3D Viewport** is a critical editor in Blender and the primary working area for **modeling, sculpting, animating, and rendering.** It offers real-time manipulation of **3D objects,** enabling users to navigate, edit, and manipulate objects within a scene.

Sections of the 3D Viewport

1. Header Region
- At the **top** of the 3D Viewport.
- Includes menus and tools like **View, Select, Add, Object, and Mode Switching.**

- Offers **immediate access to viewport settings, shading options, and snapping tools.**

2. Toolbar Region
- Located on the **left side** of the Viewport (toggle with `T`).
- Includes tools for **selection, transformation, sculpting, painting, and annotation.**
- Tool options change according to the **active mode** (e.g., **Object Mode, Edit Mode, Sculpt Mode**).

3. Sidebar Region
- On the **right side** (toggle with `N`).
- Has extra panels for **item properties, tool settings, and viewport adjustments.**
- Must be used for **accurate object manipulation and numerical transformations.**

4. Asset Shelf Region
- New feature that provides **quick access to assets, materials, and brushes.**
- Helps in **drag-and-drop** asset integration within the scene.

Startup Scene

When Blender launches, the **default scene** includes:
- A **cube** (default object).
- A **light source.**
- A **camera**.

Users can delete or modify these elements to start a new project.

Parts of the 3D Viewport

1. Object Modes

There are a number of **Object Modes** in Blender which are appropriate for various tasks:

- **Object Mode** – General object manipulation.
- **Edit Mode** – Edit mesh (vertices, edges, faces).
- **Sculpt Mode** – Computer-aided sculpting for modeling organic objects.
- **Vertex Paint / Weight Paint / Texture Paint** – Texture painting and weight map painting modes.
- **Pose Mode** – To rig and animate armatures.
- **Particle Edit Mode** – To edit particle systems like hair and fur.

Object Mode List

- In the **header** of the 3D Viewport.
- For object type switching.

Switching Objects

- Switching of objects can be done with **Outliner** or by **clicking** on the objects in the viewport.
- Select objects using `Right-click` (if Right-Click Select is used) or `Left-click` (default).

Multi-Object Editing

- More than one object can be edited **at the same time** in **Edit Mode.**
- Select more than one object, then go to **Edit Mode** (`Tab`).

Navigating the 3D Viewport

1. Navigation Basics

- **Orbit** (`Middle Mouse Button` drag) – Rotates around the scene.
- **Pan** (`Shift + Middle Mouse Button` drag) – Translates the viewport.
- **Zoom** (`Scroll Wheel` or `Ctrl + Middle Mouse Button`) – Zooms in/out.

2. Fly/Walk Navigation
- **Fly Mode** (`Shift + F`) – Translates the camera **like a first-person shooter.**
- **Walk Mode** (`Shift + F` in Camera View) – Uses arrow keys or `WASD` for movement.

3. Aligning Views
- `Numpad 1` – **Front View**
- `Numpad 3` – Right Side View
- `Numpad 7` – Top View
- `Ctrl + Numpad 1/3/7` – **Opposite View**

4. Perspective vs. Orthographic View
- **Perspective** – Objects appear with depth (realistic view).
- **Orthographic** (`Numpad 5`) – No perspective distortion (useful for technical modeling).

5. Local View
- `Numpad /` – Places an isolated object in single object editing.

6. Camera View
- `Numpad 0` – Switches to **Camera View.**
- Objects will be viewed as if they were rendered within a final render.

7. Viewpoint & View Regions

- `Shift + `~ (Tilde)` – Enables a **quick navigation menu.**
- Used for fast switching between different views.

8. Contextual Views
- Context-sensitive views **adjust automatically** based on mode and selection.

3D Cursor

1. Placement
- `Shift + Right-Click` – Moves the **3D Cursor.**
- The **3D Cursor** serves as the pivot for adding new objects.

Selecting Objects

1. Object Mode
- **Left-click** – Selects an object.
- `Shift + Left-click` – Selects multiple objects.
- `A` – Selects **all** objects.
- `Alt + A` – **Deselects** all objects.

2. Edit Mode
- Vertex Selection (`1`), Edge Selection (`2`), Face Selection (`3`)
- `Ctrl + L` – Selects **linked geometry.**

3. Pose Mode
- Used for **armature rigging** and **animating armatures.**
- `Ctrl + Tab` – Switch between **Pose Mode** and **Object Mode.**

4. Particle Edit Mode
- Used to **edit hair, fur, and other particle systems.**

Transform Controls

1. Transform Orientation
- `Global` – Translates objects in relation to **world axes.**
- `Local` – Translates objects relative to **object rotation.**
- `Normal` – Animates objects in terms of **selected component's direction.**

2. Pivot Point Options
- **Median Point** – Normal pivot (middle point of selection average).
- **3D Cursor** – Actuates the **3D Cursor** as the pivot.
- **Active Element** – Actuates most recently selected object/element.

3. Snapping
- `Shift + Tab` – Switches snapping on/off.
- Used for **precise alignment** with objects, vertices, grid, etc.

4. Proportional Editing
- `O` – Enables proportional editing (smooth transformations).
- Adjust **falloff influence** with `Scroll Wheel`.

Viewport Display & Settings

1. Object Type Visibility
- Controls visibility of **meshes, lights, cameras, and other object types.**

2. Viewport Gizmos

- Move (`G`), Rotate (`R`), Scale (`S`) Gizmos.
- `Shift + Space` – Quick tool selection.

3. Viewport Overlays

- Toggles **grid, wireframes, outlines, and other visual guides.**
- Can be accessed from the **top-right corner of the viewport.**

4. Viewport Shading Modes

- **Wireframe (`Z`, then `1`)** – Displays only object outlines.
- Simple.-Simple.-Simple.-Simple. - **Solid (`Z`, then `2`)** – Simple shading without materials.
- Simple.-Material Preview.-Simple.-Material Preview.
- **Simple** –.-Simple. - **Material Preview (`Z`, then `3`)** – Shows materials with lighting.
- Simple.-Rendered.-Simple.-Rendered.
- **Rendered (`Z`, then `4`)** – Displays final render look.

Toolbar & Sidebar Features

1. Object Mode & Edit Mode

- Simple. - Tools are changed depending on the selected mode.

2. Paint Modes

- Used for **texture painting, vertex painting, and weight painting.**

3. Grease Pencil

- Used for **2D animation and sketching** in 3D space.

4. Sidebar (`N` Key)

- **Item** – Shows object **location, rotation, scale, and dimensions.**
- **Tool** – Displays settings for the active tool.
- **View** – Controls **clipping, focal length, and 3D cursor placement.**

Viewport Rendering
- **Viewport Render** is rendering without rendering engine switch.
- Can be accessed from **View > Viewport Render Image.**

The **3D Viewport** is the **centerpiece of Blender,** with immense power tools for **modeling, sculpting, animation, and rendering.** Mastery of **navigation, selection, and transformation** will make workflow and efficiency exponentially improved.

Using the 3D Viewport on Blender 4.4:

The **3D Viewport** is the main workspace in Blender, where users are able to manipulate their **3D scene** for modeling, animating, sculpting, and texture painting. It enables real-time manipulation of objects and the environment and is a crucial part of the Blender workflow.

Header Region

The **Header** is positioned at the top of the 3D Viewport and contains **menus and controls** that differ based on the active mode. It is divided into three sections:

1. Mode & Menus

- **Mode Selection (`Ctrl + Tab`)** – Switches between different **Object Modes,** such as **Edit Mode, Sculpt Mode, Pose Mode, and more.**
- **Quick Mode Switching (`Tab`)** – Toggles between **Object Mode and Edit Mode** for the supported objects.
- **Pie Menu (`Ctrl + Tab`)** – Enables fast access to different **modes**.
- **Pose Mode** – If an **Armature** is selected, `Ctrl + Tab` toggles between **Object Mode and Pose Mode.**

2. View Menu

- Offers **navigating the 3D space** tools.
- Offers various **view options,** like **Perspective, Orthographic, and Camera View.**

3. Object Mode Menus

These menus are present in **Object Mode** and vary with the current mode:

- Select – Object selection tools.
- **Add (`Shift + A`)** – Allows adding new objects like **meshes, lights, cameras, and others.**
- **Object** – Object manipulation tools, such as **duplicating, deleting, and parenting.**
- **Right-click Menu** – Offers easy access to frequently used object tools.

1. Transform Orientation (`Comma`)
- Modifies the **gizmo's orientation of the transform,** impacting rotation and translation.

2. Pivot Point (`Period`)
- Determines the **pivot point** for transformations, affecting rotation and scaling of objects.

3. Snapping (`Shift + Tab`)
- Enables **snapping** to precisely align with **objects, grid, or vertices.**
- Holding `Ctrl` for a moment **enables/disables snapping** temporarily.

4. Proportional Editing (`O`)
- Gradually deforms **surrounding unselected items** along with selected items.
- Handy for organic modeling and terrain sculpting.

Display & Shading Options

1. Object Type Visibility
- Controls which **object types** (meshes, lights, cameras, etc.) are **visible and selectable.**

2. Viewport Gizmos
- Toggles the visibility of the move, rotate, and scale gizmos.

3. Viewport Overlays

- Adjusts grid, wireframe, and selection outlines.

4. X-Ray (`Alt + Z`)
- **Places objects in semi-transparent mode,** which allows for occluded elements selection.
- When in **Pose Mode,** X-Ray displays **Armature visibly all the time,** even hiding behind other objects.

5. Viewport Shading: Is responsible for **how objects get rendered in the 3D Viewport:**
- **Wireframe (`Z`, then `1`)** – Shows only lines.
- **Solid (`Z`, then `2`)** – Shading without the use of materials.
- **Material Preview (`Z`, then `3`)** – Shows materials and lighting.
- **Rendered (`Z`, then `4`)** – Presents a preview of the final rendering.

Toolbar Region

1. The Toolbar region is Situated on the **left side** (toggle with `T`).
2. It has Has **varying tools based on the mode,** including:
- Modeling tools in **Edit Mode.**
3. **Brush tools** in Sculpt Mode.
- Texture painting tools in **Paint Modes.**

Sidebar Region (`N` Key)

- Located on the **right side** (toggle with `N`).
- Displays additional **properties** for:

   - **Active object** – Location, rotation, scale, and dimensions.

- **Active tool** – Settings for the selected tool.

- **Viewport settings** – Settings for **clipping, focal length, and 3D cursor location.**

Asset Shelf Region

- It appears in **certain modes** (e.g., **Pose Mode, Sculpt Mode**).
- It offers **immediate access to assets,** including:

  - Pose assets for animation and rigging.
  - Brush assets for painting and sculpting.

The **3D Viewport** is Blender's **main workspace, with fantastically powerful functionality for navigating, editing, and rendering.** Mastering its **header, toolbars, and display settings** will enhance your workflow and productivity.

CHAPTER 16

EXPLORING THE STARTUP SCENE, AND OBJECT MODES IN BLENDER 4.4

The Startup Scene

Once you launch Blender and close the **splash screen,** the **Startup Scene** appears in the **3D Viewport**—unless another **different blend file** is launched. This **default scene** is a starting point to start creating and editing 3D material. It can be **setup** to your workflow.

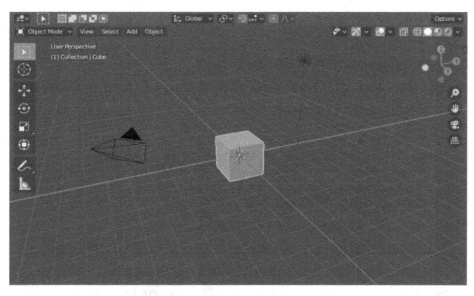

The startup scene.

Parts of the Startup Scene

The **Startup Scene** contains a set of basic elements:

1. Cube (Default Mesh Object)
- The **gray cube** in the center is a **basic 3D object.**
- Its **orange border** indicates that it is **selected**.
- The **small orange dot** at its center represents its **Origin**, which points to its **exact location in 3D space.**

2. Light (Illumination Source)
- Represented by **concentric black circles.**
- Provides **lighting** to the scene, to allow objects to be viewed when rendered.
- Different **kinds of light** (Point, Sun, Spot, Area) may be inserted or modified.

3. Camera (Viewpoint for Rendering)
- Represented as a **pyramid with a large triangle at the top.**
- Determines the viewpoint under which to render images and animation.
- Press `Numpad 0` to **look through the camera.**

4. 3D Cursor (Object Placement Tool)
- A cross with a red-and-white circle.
- Determines where **new objects** are placed when added.
- Can also be used as a **pivot point for transformations.**
- `Shift + Right Click` moves the **3D Cursor** to a new position.

5. Grid Floor

- A **gray set of lines** which form a **floor** at **zero height** in the 3D world.
- The **red and green lines** are the **X and Y axes** of the **world coordinate system.**
- The **point where the lines intersect** is the **World Origin (0,0,0),** which is also the **origin of the default Cube.**
- - Grid settings can be adjusted in **Viewport Overlays** (`View > Viewport Overlays`).

6. Text Info (Viewport Information Display)

- Located in the **top-left corner** of the viewport.
- Displays useful **scene information,** such as:
  - Number of objects in the scene
  - Memory usage
  - Active tool details
- Can be adjusted via **Viewport Overlays settings.**

Customizing the Startup Scene

Blender enables users to **alter the default startup scene** to suit their workflow:

1. Make Changes
- **Add or delete objects,** alter lighting, modify camera settings, or change viewport settings.

2. Save as Default (`File > Defaults > Save Startup File`)
- To modify and then **save the default startup scene,** go to File > Defaults > Save Startup File to **overwrite the default scene.**
- On the subsequent Blender startup, Blender will apply your customized setup.

The **Startup Scene** is a simple framework for Blender users, with a **Cube, Light, Camera, 3D Cursor, and Grid Floor** as fundamental tools. Familiarity with these elements will assist you in **orienting in the 3D Viewport** and start working efficiently.

Understanding Object Modes in Blender 4.4:

Object Modes in Blender determine how you interact with objects within the **3D Viewport.** Each mode serves a specific purpose, varying from object transformation to sculpting, painting, and posing.

You can toggle between modes through the **Mode Selector** in the **3D Viewport header,** or through the **Ctrl + Tab** keyboard shortcut to offer a **pie menu** access. The **Tab** key cycles **Edit Mode** on objects that support it.

Types of Object Modes

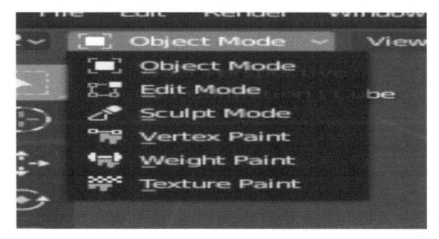

The Mode select menu.

All object types in Blender have modes that vary from one object type to another. What follows is the breakdown of all the available modes:

1. Object Mode (Default)
- Used for positioning, rotating, scaling, duplicating, and managing objects.
- Available for **all object types.**

2. Edit Mode
- Used for **modifying an object's shape** (e.g., moving vertices, edges, and faces for meshes).
- Available for meshes, curves, surfaces, text, and Grease Pencil objects.
- Shortcut: **Tab.**

3. Sculpt Mode
- Provides **brush-based tools** for sculpting organic shapes.
- Is applicable for **meshes and Grease Pencil objects.**

4. Vertex Paint Mode
- Used for **painted vertex colors directly on a mesh**.
- Is applicable for **meshes and Grease Pencil objects.**

5. Weight Paint Mode
- Used to **paint weight values to vertices,** typically for rigging and animation.
- Comes with **meshes and Grease Pencil objects.**

6. Texture Paint Mode
- Facilitates the painting **directly on to a 3D object of texture.**
- Operates only with **meshes.**

7. Particle Edit Mode

- Can be used **for editing particle systems**, including **hair grooming**.
- Works for **mesh with particle system.**

8. Pose Mode

- Used to **pose armatures (rigs)** for character animation.
- Available for **armatures only.**

9. Draw Mode (Grease Pencil)

- Dedicated to **drawing Grease Pencil strokes.**
- Available for **Grease Pencil objects only.**

10. Sculpt Mode (Grease Pencil)

- Used for **deforming Grease Pencil strokes organically.**
- Available for **Grease Pencil objects only.**

11. Edit Mode (Grease Pencil)

- Employed for **editing Grease Pencil strokes and points.**
- Accessible only for **Grease Pencil objects.**

How Object Modes Affect Blender

- **Toolbar & Shortcuts:** Every mode has its own **set of tools** and **keyboard shortcuts.**
- **Viewport Appearance:** Certain modes, such as **Weight Paint Mode,** modify how objects are viewed.
- **Other Editors:** Some editors, like the **UV Editor,** must be in a special mode (e.g., Edit Mode).

Switching Objects Without Exiting a Mode

Blender will automatically change to **Object Mode** when you click on another object. But you can switch objects without exiting the same mode:

1. Using the Outliner:
The Outliner displays a **dot** next to objects that support the active mode.
- Click on this **dot** to switch to that object **without leaving the mode.**

2. **Alt + Q (Shortcut):**
- Move to another object in the **3D Viewport** and hit **Alt + Q** to switch to it **without leaving the mode.**

Multi-Object Editing

Certain modes, i.e., **Edit Mode** and **Pose Mode**, allow editing **multiple objects at a time:**

Entering Multi-Object Mode:
1. Initially, **choose multiple objects** before entering the mode.
2. Then, enter the desired mode.

Adding More Objects to an Active Mode:
- **Ctrl + Left Click** on the **dot** in the Outliner to delete/include objects from the mode.

Notes: The Properties Editor displays only information for the **active object.**

- You **cannot** create edges between vertices of **different objects.**

It is necessary to understand **Object Modes** in order to be efficient in Blender. Every mode is for a specific **workflow,** modeling, sculpting, animation, or painting. Understanding how to change between objects in a mode and how to use multi-object editing can **speed up your workflow** by far.

CHAPTER 17:

NAVIGATION TECHNIQUES IN BLENDER

Effective working in the 3D space of Blender requires learning to navigate. Since Blender operates in three-dimensional space, you need to learn how to move around, shift your view, and control the manner in which you view objects in the scene. This is a chapter on navigating the 3D Viewport, but the same principles apply to other editors, such as the Image Editor, where you can pan and zoom as well.

In order to achieve the full potential of Blender's navigation tools, it's essential to understand how to rotate, pan, and zoom in the scene and how to use these functions like the navigation gizmo, camera view, and local view. Blender comes with multiple navigation options so that users can choose what feels most comfortable to them—be it the mouse, keyboard shortcuts, or the on-screen gizmo.

Tip: Certain navigation devices require a middle mouse button or numpad. If your computer lacks these, refer to Blender's **Keyboard and Mouse settings** for alternatives to doing things.

Navigation Gizmo

Blender features a **Navigation Gizmo,** a supporting on-screen tool accessible in the top right of the 3D Viewport. The gizmo allows you to manipulate your scene visually without necessarily having to use keyboard shortcuts.

Navigation Gizmo (left) and Navigation Gizmo in camera view (right).

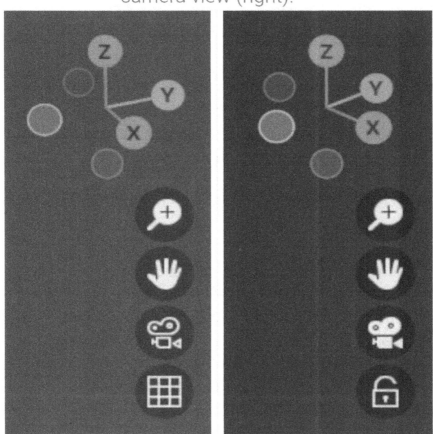

Understanding the Navigation Gizmo

Navigation Gizmo consists of a few parts:

- Orbit Gizmo:

- The **colored sphere with axis labels (X, Y, Z)** is your current state of the 3D View.
- Click and drag on it using the **Left Mouse Button (LMB)** to rotate the view (orbit the state).
- A label of one of the axes (X, Y, or Z) is clicked to orient the view along that axis.
- The same axis label is clicked again to reverse the view to the opposite side.

Navigation Buttons Below the Gizmo:

Four additional buttons are located below the Orbit Gizmo, each of which performs a specific task:

1. **Zoom View** – Controls the zoom factor in the 3D Viewport.
2. **Pan View** – Moves the camera's view position to the left or right or up or down.
3. **Toggle Camera View** – Switches to see what the active camera sees.
4. **Toggle Projection Mode** – Activates and deactivates perspective and orthographic view.
   - In **Camera View,** this button also turns "**Lock Camera to View**" mode on and off, allowing you to move the camera dynamically.

Once you master the Navigation Gizmo, you can navigate through your scene easily with ease and less time required, improving productivity in the workflow and making object manipulation simpler.

Methods of Navigation

Apart from using the Navigation Gizmo, Blender also offers several manual methods by which you can place your view within the 3D space. They include orbiting, rolling, panning, zooming, and framing objects. With these, you are able to perform precise explorations and manipulations of your scene.

1. Orbiting the View

Orbit allows you to move around the scene and observe objects at angles other than those you'd normally observe while sitting in a specific position with regard to them. It is useful while modeling, sculpting, or looking at an object from all sides.

- Method 1: Using the Mouse
- Hold down the **middle mouse button (MMB)** and use the mouse to pan around the scene.

- Method 2: Using the Keyboard
- Press **NumPad 4** or **NumPad 6** to orbit **horizontally** (left/right).
- Press **NumPad 8** or **NumPad 2** to orbit **vertically** (up/down).

- Method 3: Using the Navigation Gizmo
- Click and drag the **Orbit Gizmo** (top right of the 3D Viewport).

Tip: In case your mouse lacks a middle button, you can enable **"Emulate 3 Button Mouse"** in Blender Preferences to use **Alt + LMB** as a substitute.

2. Rolling the View

Rolling is used to slightly rotate the view around the screen's axis, which is useful to align objects onto a fresh view.

- **Shortcut:** Roll the view left or right with **Shift + NumPad 4** or **Shift + NumPad 6.**

3. Panning the View

Panning is utilized to move the view completely left, right, up, or down without changing the camera angle.

- Method 1: Using the Mouse
- Press **Shift + MMB** and move the mouse.

- Method 2: Using the Keyboard
- Press **Shift + NumPad 8/2/4/6** to pan in other directions.

- Method 3: Using the Navigation Gizmo
- Press the **Pan View** button underneath the Orbit Gizmo.

Panning comes in handy while working on huge objects or detailing areas of interest within a scene.

4. Zooming In and Out

Zooming lets you zoom in to an object or zoom out for a broad overview.

- Method 1: Using the Mouse Scroll Wheel
- Scroll **up** to zoom in.
- Scroll **down** to zoom out.

- Method 2: Using the Keyboard
- Press **Ctrl + NumPad 2/8** to zoom in and out incrementally.

- Method 3: Using the Navigation Gizmo

- Click the **Zoom View** button.

- Method 4: Zoom Region (Precision Zooming)
- Press **Shift + B,** then draw a box around the region to zoom in on.

Tip: If zooming is lagging or is too sensitive, alter the zoom speed in the **Preferences > Navigation Settings.**

5. Dolly View (Smooth Zooming)
Dolly View makes zooming more natural, emulating the way a real-world camera would move.

- **Shortcut**: Hold **Ctrl + MMB** and move the mouse forward or backward.
- This is more controllable than using the scroll wheel.

6. Centering Objects in View
When dealing with multiple objects, it is helpful to bring the view centered on a specific object.

Frame All (Highlight Everything in the Scene)
- Press **Home** to reset the view and align all objects back in the viewport.

Frame Selected (Highlight a Single Object)
- Select an object and press **NumPad. (period)** to zoom in on the selected object.

Frame Last Stroke (For Grease Pencil Users)

- Press **Alt + Home** to center on the most recent Grease Pencil stroke.

These shortcut frames save you a lot of time when creating large or complicated scenes.

7. Fly/Walk Navigation

View Navigation.

Blender has an interactive way of navigation as if you were within a computer object. There are two modes:

Walk Navigation

- Moves in a wire-framed first-person computer game style.
- Controls
- **WASD keys** for movement.
- **Mouse Look** to change direction.
- **Spacebar** to teleport to a location.
- **Press Esc or Right Click** to leave Walk Mode.

Fly Navigation

- Moves as if flying like a drone, with complete control of speed and direction.

- Controls:
- **Camera movement** with the mouse.
  - **Scroll wheel** for speed adjustment.
  - **LMB to accept** or **RMB to reject.**

Shortcut to Turn On: Press **Shift + F** to enable Fly Mode.

These modes of navigation are particularly convenient for viewing big environments or establishing camera angles dynamically.

8. Aligning the View
Aligning the view can prove useful when working with some angles or views.

Perspective & Orthographic View Switching

Blender offers the option to switch between **Perspective View (3D depth)** and **Orthographic View (flat projection).**

Orthographic projection.

Perspective projection.

- **Shortcut**: Press **NumPad 5** to switch modes.

Tip: Orthographic View is useful for precise modeling, while Perspective View is more intuitive for regular navigating.

If you're interested, look at the following paragraph.

9. Local View (Isolating Objects)
Local View enables you to concentrate on one object by temporarily hiding all else.

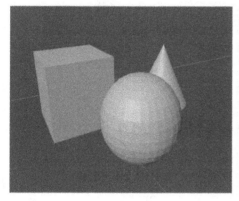

Global View.   Local View.

Shortcut: Press **NumPad / (slash)** to turn Local View on/off.
- It is useful for precise modeling without distraction.

10. Camera View & Positioning

Looking at your scene from the camera's point of view assists in setting up renders.

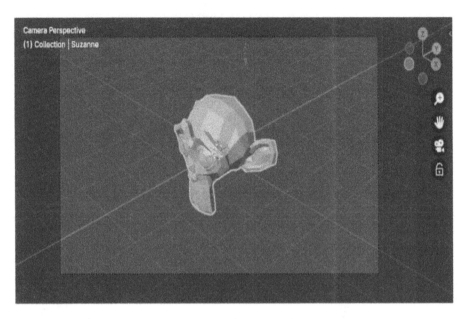

Demonstration of camera view.

- Viewing Through the Camera: Press **NumPad 0.**
- Lock Camera to View:
- Enable View > Lock Camera to View in the Sidebar.
- Now, an action like moving the viewport will also move the camera.

Setting the Active Camera

If you have more than one, select one and press **Ctrl + NumPad 0** to activate it.

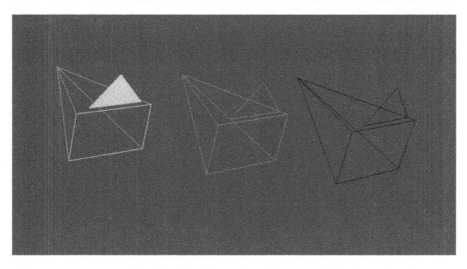

Active camera (left) displayed with a solid triangle above it.

Frame Camera Bounds

- Use **Shift + NumPad 0** to view the render frame precisely.

Zoom Camera 1:1 (Pixel Accuracy)

- Use **Shift + NumPad 0,** and then press **F12** to render.
- This will have you view the scene at actual pixel resolution.

Viewpoint Shortcuts (Quick Camera Alignments)

Blender provides you with hotkeys to align straight away to different views.

- **NumPad 1** → Front View
- **NumPad 3** → Right View
- **NumPad 7** → Top View
- **NumPad 9** → Opposite View (Back/Left/Bottom)

Tip: Keep **Ctrl** pressed and click these shortcuts for the opposite side (e.g., **Ctrl + NumPad 1 = Back View).**

View Regions & Clipping

Blender allows you to control how much of the scene is being displayed.

Region/Volume clipping.

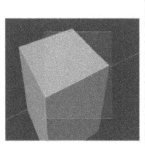
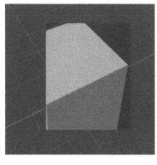

Selecting a region.

Region selected.

View rotated.

- **Clipping Region:** Limits the part of the view to be viewed from a scene.
- **Render Region:** Allows you to render only a section of the viewport that you have specified.

Render region and associated render.

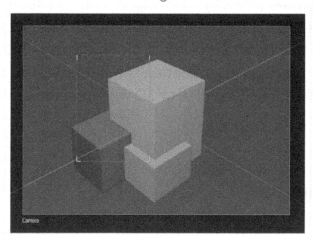 

Quad View (Split Screen Navigation)

Quad View separates the screen into **four views (Top, Front, Right, and Perspective).**

Shortcut: Toggle Quad View on and off with **Ctrl + Alt + Q.**
- It is convenient for accurate modeling.

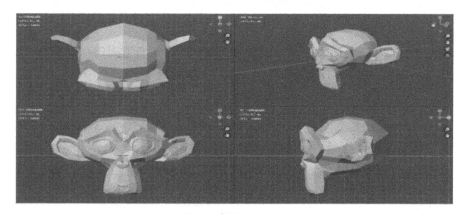

Quad View.

Mastering navigation in Blender makes you so much more productive. No matter if you use shortcuts, the Navigation Gizmo, or interactive modes like Fly/Walk Navigation, all these tools provide you with the convenience of navigating through your scene. The better you know the techniques, the more fluid and natural your 3D work processes will be.

The 3D Cursor in Blender

The **3D Cursor** is a fundamental part of Blender that is used as a reference point within 3D space. It possesses a **location and rotation,** and because of this, it can be utilized in numerous different ways:

- It dictates where **new objects** that are added are positioned in the scene.
- It is used as a reference for **object transformation** by orienting the pivot point or transform orientation.
- It is needed for certain modeling tools, such as the **Bend tool**, which uses the cursor as an anchor.

Being able to control the **3D Cursor** gives you greater control over object placement, transformations, and precision modeling.

Positioning the 3D Cursor

There are several ways to place the **3D Cursor** where you wish it to be.

1. Placing the 3D Cursor with the Mouse Directly

The simplest way to place the **3D Cursor** where you wish it to be is to click in the 3D Viewport where you wish it to be.

Using the Cursor Tool

- **Mode:** Can be used in **Object Mode, Edit Mode, and Pose Mode.**
- **Tool:** Cursor (located in the Toolbar).
- **Shortcut:** Shift + Right Mouse Button (RMB).

To apply it:

1. Choose the **Cursor Tool** from the **Toolbar** (left viewport).
2. Click anywhere on the scene using the **Left Mouse Button (LMB).**
3. The **3D Cursor** will shift to the exact spot you clicked.

Adjusting Cursor Orientation

By default, the **3D Cursor orientation** will match the view that you're currently working in, but you can change this within the **Tool Settings:**

- Set it to **the surface normal** of the currently selected object.
- Make it match **the transform orientation of an object.**

Making Quick Placement with Shift + RMB

Instead of needing to go through the motions of choosing the Cursor Tool directly, you can simply use **Shift + RMB** whenever.

- The **3D Cursor** will jump to the location clicked.
- It will be aligned to the **view orientation,** and thus it is perfect for fast placements.

2. Precise Placement with Orthogonal Views

For **accurate placement,** using **several orthogonal views** is recommended.

- Open two orthogonal **orthogonal 3D Viewports** (e.g., **Top, Front, and Side Views**).
- This allows you to **control the positioning on two axes in one view** while setting the **depth in another.**

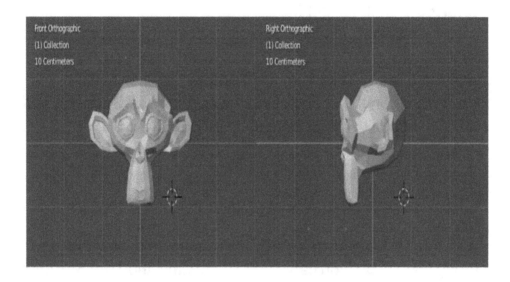

Positioning the 3D Cursor with two orthogonal views.

Use the NumPad keys to switch views:
- **NumPad 7** → Top View
- **NumPad 1** → Front View
- **NumPad 3** → Side View

This method is very useful when working with complex models that require highly specific placements.

Tip: Blender will automatically consider depth of geometry under the cursor. If you want to disable this, you can toggle **Cursor Surface Project** in the **Preferences.**

3. Manually positioning the 3D Cursor via the Sidebar
The **Sidebar Panel** offers a different way to manually set the **3D Cursor's** position and orientation.

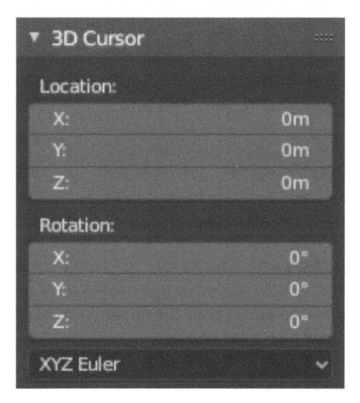

The 3D Cursor panel of the Sidebar region.

- **Mode**: Exists in All Modes.
- **Location**: Found at Sidebar > View Tab > 3D Cursor Panel.
- Shortcut to Show Sidebar: Use **N.**

You are able to perform the following in this panel:
- Enter **exact coordinates** for the **location of the 3D Cursor** (X, Y, Z coordinates).
- Select the **angles of rotation** to place the cursor in exactly the right location.

This technique is perfect for when you require **mathematical precision** instead of visual positioning.

4. Snapping the 3D Cursor for Precision Placement
Blender also has **snapping modes** that enable you to precisely place the **3D Cursor** in relation to other objects.

Using the Snap Menu
- **Mode:** Available in Object Mode, Edit Mode, and Pose Mode.
- **Menu Path:** Object / Mesh / Curve / Armature → Snap → Cursor to …
- **Shortcut: Shift + S**

The **3D Cursor** can be rapidly moved from this menu to:
- The **origin** of a selected object.
- The center of a selected face, edge, or vertex.
- A **specific point in the scene** based on selected elements.

Snap Menu Usage
- **Cursor to World Origin:** Sends the cursor back to (0,0,0).

- **Cursor to Selected:** Places the cursor at the center of the current object.
- **Cursor to Grid:** Snaps the cursor to the nearest grid point to align precisely.

Tip: Snapping offers **precise alignment**, particularly useful for snapping objects to either side of an axis, centering objects symmetrically, or snapping them against key reference points.

The **3D Cursor** is a very powerful tool that enables exact object placement, transformation, and snapping in Blender. By becoming proficient in its various positioning techniques—**direct mouse placement, orthogonal view adjustments, sidebar input, and snapping**—you can work more effectively and maintain **accurate** object positions in your 3D scenes.

To work effectively within Blender's 3D space, you need to be a navigation master. This is simply a matter of navigating around the scene and adjusting your view with ease. While this chapter concerns the **3D Viewport**, the same navigation rules apply to other editors within Blender, such as the **Image Editor**, where you can pan and zoom as previously described.

Tip: Some navigation operations require a **middle mouse button (MMB)** or a **numpad**. If these are not found on your machine, see Blender's **Keyboard and Mouse Settings** for an alternative control.

Navigation Gizmo
Blender contains a **Navigation Gizmo** in the top-right corner of the **3D Viewport,** and it is a convenient way to control your view.

Understanding the Navigation Gizmo

The gizmo contains:

1. **Orbit Controls** – A sphere that is labeled with an axis marker.
   - **Click & Drag:** Rotates the view (orbits).
   - **Click on a Label of an Axis:** Rotates the view to align with the chosen axis.
   - **Click a Second Time:** Jumps the view to the opposite side of the selected axis.

2. **Navigation Buttons Below the Gizmo:**
   - **Zoom In/Out** – Alters the magnification of the viewport.
   - **Pan** – Pans the entire view of the viewport left-right or up-down.
   - **Toggle Camera View** – Switches between the user's view and the current active camera view.
   - **Projection Toggle** – Toggles between **Perspective** and **Orthographic** views. While in **Camera View,** this button turns on or off **Lock Camera to View** mode.

3D Cursor: Your Anchor Point in 3D Space

The **3D Cursor** is a key tool in Blender used as a point of reference within 3D space. Both **position (location)** and **rotation (orientation)** exist, and it is used for various purposes such as:
- Setting where new objects are located.
- Serving as a pivot point for transformations.
- Serving as a reference point for tools like the **Bend Modifier.**

Location of the 3D Cursor

You can locate the **3D Cursor** in a number of different ways:

1. Direct Position with the Mouse
- **Tool: Cursor Tool** (found in the Toolbar).
- **Shortcut:** `Shift + Right Mouse Button (RMB)`.

How it Works:
- Select the **Cursor Tool** and left-click (LMB) anywhere in the scene in order to move the **3D Cursor.**
- The cursor aligns automatically with the view by default. However, you may have it line up with a surface normal or the orientation of an object transformation.

Precision Tip: To position in **precise** location, use two perpendicular **orthographic views** (e.g., **Top (`Numpad 7`), Front (`Numpad 1`),** or **Side (`Numpad 3`))**. This is a method by which you may have precise positioning along different axes.

2. Positioning via Sidebar
- **Panel:** Sidebar → View → 3D Cursor
- You may input highly accurate location and rotation values manually in the **Sidebar** to position the cursor with high accuracy.

3. Snapping the Cursor to Objects
- **Shortcut:** `Shift + S` (Opens the **Snap Menu**)
- **Functionality:** This allows you to snap the cursor to specific reference points, i.e.:
- The center of a chosen object.
  - The midpoint of a chosen edge or face.
  - A vertex or an object's origin.

Tip: If you must turn off automatic snapping to geometry, switch the **Cursor Surface Project** option in Preferences.

Selecting Objects in Blender

Selection is fundamental to Blender operation. The **3D Viewport** possesses some selection tools, along with the overall selection methods found in Blender's **Interface Section.**

Selection Shortcuts and Menus
- **Select by Origin (`Ctrl`)** – Picks objects based on their **origin point** as opposed to their shape.
- **Selection Menu (`Alt`)** – When you've got multiple objects with your mouse over them, it helps you choose the one you need.
- **Combine `Ctrl + Alt`** – Displays a **selection menu** based on **object origins.**

Selection Modes Based on Object Type

Selection in Blender occurs in different manners, depending on what you are working with:
- **Object Mode:** You apply it to select entire objects.
- **Edit Mode:** Enables selection and editing of elements within an object (vertices, edges, faces).
- **Pose Mode:** For selection and manipulation of bones in an armature.
- **Other Edit Modes:** Curve Edit Mode, Metaball Edit Mode, Grease Pencil Edit Mode, Lattice Edit Mode, and others.

Transform Orientation: Controlling Object Movement

In Blender, **Transform Orientation** controls how objects or selected items orient when they are transformed. This directly affects how you move, resize, or rotate objects.

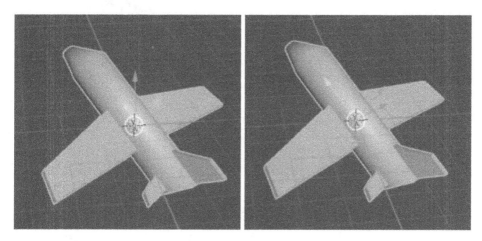

With the default Global transform orientation (left) it's tricky to move the plane in the direction it's facing, but with Local (right) it's easy.

How to Change Transform Orientation

- **Shortcut:** `Comma (,)`
- **Location:** 3D Viewport Header → Transform Orientation Menu

- **Alternative Method:** Temporary axis locking (`G → X → X` to switch between Global and Local X-axis).

Transform Orientations Types

1. **Global** – Has transformations align to Blender's world axes (**X, Y, Z**).
2. **Local** – Has transformations align based on the orientation of the active object.
3. **Normal** – In **Edit Mode,** has transformations align to the normal direction of the selected element. In **Object Mode,** it behaves as Local.
4. **Gimbal** – Makes an object's **Rotation Mode,** a representation of how Euler rotations affect axes.
5. **View** – Aligns transformations to the current viewport view.
6. **Cursor** – Uses the orientation of the **3D Cursor** as the transformation reference.
7. **Parent** – Aligns transformations to the object's **parent**.

Example: When you incline an object and use **Global** orientation, it will move in a stiff X, Y, or Z direction. But with **Local**, there will be movement in the direction of the rotation of the object.

Cube with the rotation gizmo active in multiple transform orientations.

Default cube with Global transform orientation selected.

Rotated cube with Global orientation, gizmo has not changed.

Local orientation, gizmo matches the object's rotation.

Normal orientation, in Edit Mode.

Gimbal transform orientation.

View transform orientation.

Parent transform orientation. Cube parented to rotated empty.

Creating Custom Transform Orientations

Blender also allows you to create your own transformation orientations for special purposes.

Transform Orientation panel.

How to Create a Custom Orientation

1. Select an object or mesh element.
2. Go to the **Transform Orientation Panel** in the **3D Viewport Header.**
3. Click on the **"+\" button** to add a new custom orientation.
4. Rename the new orientation (named after the active object by default).

Customization Options:
- **Use View:** Sets the new orientation to match the viewport.

319

- **Use After Creation:** Defaults to the new orientation automatically.
- **Overwrite Previous:** In case of a name clash, Blender adds a suffix except when you tick this option and overwrite the earlier orientation.

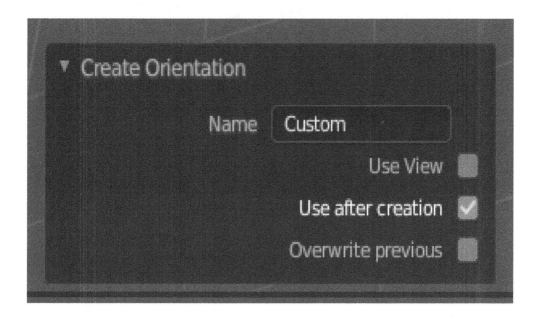

Deleting a Custom Orientation

To remove an orientation, select it from the list and press the **"×"** **button.**

Mastering navigation and transformation in Blender is vital to efficient workflow. Whether you're relocating the **3D Cursor,** selecting objects, or handling transformations, mastering these tools top and bottom will make working in Blender significantly easier. Mastering these functions and incorporating them into your needs will allow you to gain greater control over your 3D spaces and be more effective in using Blender.

CHAPTER 18

WORKING WITH PIVOT POINT IN BLENDER

In Blender, the **Pivot Point** is defined as the point where transformations - rotation and scaling take place. It is really an important setting for precision modeling, animation, and object manipulation. Knowing all pivot types and how to correctly set them can really amplify your workflow by making transformations easier and more intuitive.

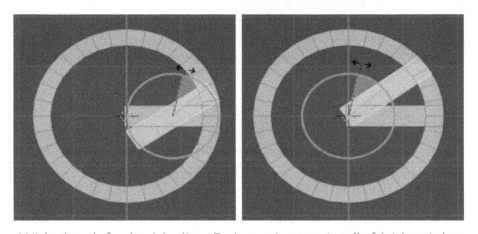

With the default «Median Point» pivot point (left) it's tricky to bring the second wheel spoke into place, but with «3D Cursor» (right) it's easy.

How to Change the Pivot Point

To modify the **Pivot Point,** you can:

1. **Utilize the Pivot Selector in the 3D Viewport Header:**
   - Look for the **Pivot Icon** at the top left part of the **3D Viewport.**
     - Click on it and a drop-down menu will appear where you will have the option of selecting various pivot types.

2. **Use the Keyboard Shortcut:**
   - Press **Period (.)** on your keyboard to bring up the Pivot Point menu.
   - Select your desired pivot type from the given options.

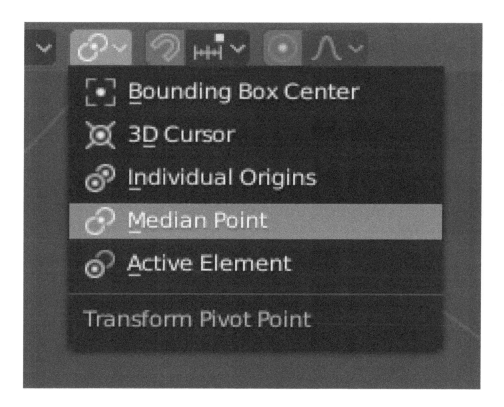

Types of Pivots in Blender

Every type of pivot has a different use and is helpful in different modeling, rigging, and animation projects. Let's explore further about each type.

Bounding Box Center

Bounding Box Center places pivot at the very center of 3D Viewport object, or selected part, into the smallest conceivable imaginary box. The box may enclose said object or group of elements being selected.

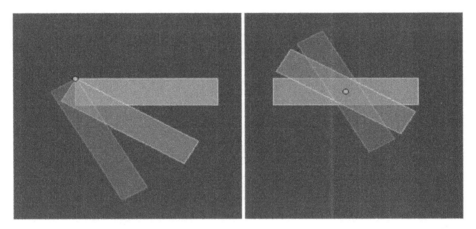

Single object rotation.

How to Set-Up Bounding Box Center

- Enter 3D Viewport
- Click, within the headers of 3D Viewport, on **" Pivot Sellector "**.
- From the sub-menu, chose **" BOunding Box Centre "**.

- Or else, hit Period (.) → Bounding Box Center from the keyboard.

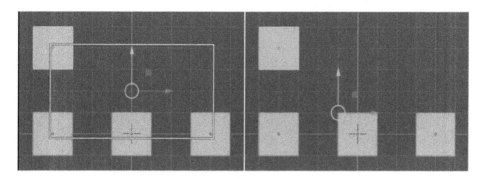

Difference between «Bounding Box Center» (left) and
«Median Point» (right).

When to Use It:
- Whenever you need **even transformations** for the whole object.
- Good for **symmetrical scaling** (like scaling a model of a house, keeping the proportions balanced).

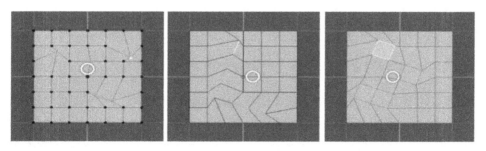

The effects of rotation in different mesh selection modes.
The pivot point is shown by a yellow circle.

- For use in **group selections** under **Edit Mode,** to apply changes around the middle part of the selection.

How to Keep It:

- Ensure your model is organized properly so the **bounding box center** is a useful point of reference at all times.

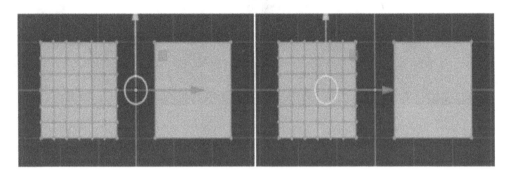

Difference between «Bounding Box Center» (left) and «Median Point» (right).

- Undo transformations (**Ctrl + A → Apply Scale/Rotation/Location**) if the bounding box fails to behave.

3D Cursor (Precision Control)

The **3D Cursor** can serve as a **custom pivot point** by which you can rotate, scale, and move objects from around a point within the scene. It's great for making **precise manipulations** in situations where the default pivot tools won't cut it.

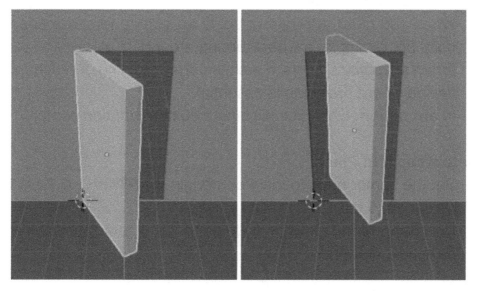

Rotation around the 3D Cursor compared to the Median
Point.

How to Set It Up 3D Cursor for Precision Control:

To start, place the **3D Cursor** where you wish to place the pivot point:
- **Manually:** Select the **Cursor Tool** from the **Toolbar** and left-click anywhere in the scene.
- **With a shortcut:** Use Shift + Right Mouse Button (Shift + RMB).
- **With numerical input:** Press **N** to open the **Sidebar**, navigate to the **View tab**, and set precise cursor coordinates under **3D Cursor.**
- Make 3D Cursor active as Pivot:

  - Click the **Pivot Selector** in the 3D Viewport Header and select **3D Cursor.**
  - Or, use the shortcut **Period (.) → 3D Cursor.**

When to Use It Effectively:
- When you need to rotate or scale an object around a specific point (for example, a wheel turning around its axle).
- When snapping objects in architectural modeling or mechanical design where precision is essential.
- In **animation,** while establishing a custom rotation center.

How to Keep It In Place:
- Set the cursor back to the world origin with **Shift + C** (sets the cursor on (0,0,0)).
- Use **Snap Menu (Shift + S)** to snap the cursor to an object, a selection, or a grid.

Individual Origins (Independent Transformations)

In **Individual Origins,** each individual object (that you have selected in **Object Mode)** or mesh piece (that you selected in **Edit Mode**) rotates around its own pivot rather than a common pivot. This is great when you want to scale or rotate certain objects independently of others.

Setting Up Individual Origins:

- Click the Pivot Selector in the 3D Viewport Header.
- Choose Individual Origins.
- Or press the shortcut Period (.) → Individual Origins.

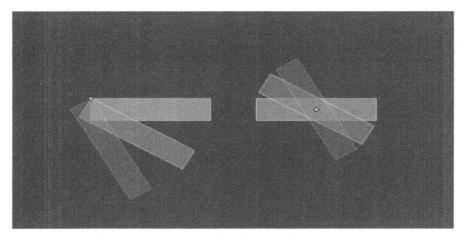

Rotation around individual origins.

When to Use It:

- For modeling with various objects and need them to rotate, scale, or move on their own (e.g., rotating several planets around their individual axes).

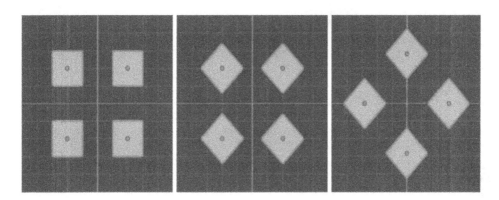

Starting situation, rotation around Individual Origins, rotation around Median Point.

- When modeling intricate structures where each part needs to be worked on independently.

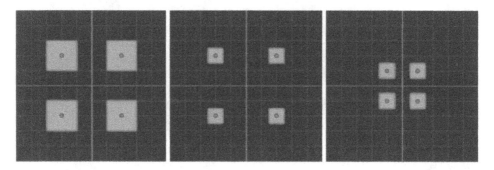

Starting situation, scaling using Individual Origins, scaling using Median Point.

- When scaling or rotating individual parts of a mesh without combining their movements.

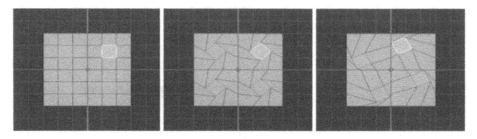

Starting situation, rotation around Individual Origins, rotation around Median Point.

Starting situation, scaling using Individual Origins, scaling using Median Point.

How to Achieve It:

- Have objects with **proper origin points** defined. Use Object →
  Set Origin to reposition their pivots.
- If objects are moving in a strange way, inspect for unwanted
  parent-child relationships in the **Outliner**.

Median Point (Default Setting)

The **Median Point** puts the pivot at the **average location** of all the
chosen objects or elements. It gives a balanced transformation and
is, therefore, an excellent all-around pivot setting.

How to Set It Up Median Point:

- Click on the Pivot Selector in the 3D Viewport Header.
- Select **Median Point.**

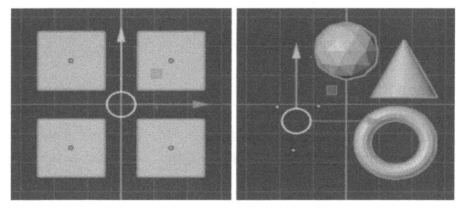

Median points in Object Mode.

- Or press the shortcut Period (.) → Median Point.

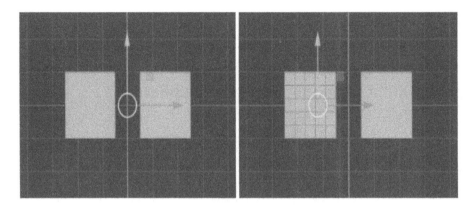

Median points in Edit Mode.

When to Use It:
- When performing balanced transformations on multiple objects or mesh selections.
- When performing group scaling or rotations, for instance, rotating a group of pillars about their center.
- Suits **proportional editing** best, where corrections are to be distributed proportionally.

How to Keep It:
- If transformations do not go as anticipated, check if objects have different **scales or rotations.**
- Clean transformations with Ctrl + A → Apply Scale/Rotation/Location.

Active Element (Precise Alignment)

The **Active Element** makes the pivot at the **last selected** object or mesh element. It comes in handy when you want to transform around a certain item in your selection.

How to Set It Up:

- Click the Pivot Selector in the 3D Viewport Header.
- Choose Active Element.

Starting point, rotation, and scaling.

- Or use the shortcut Period (.) → Active Element.

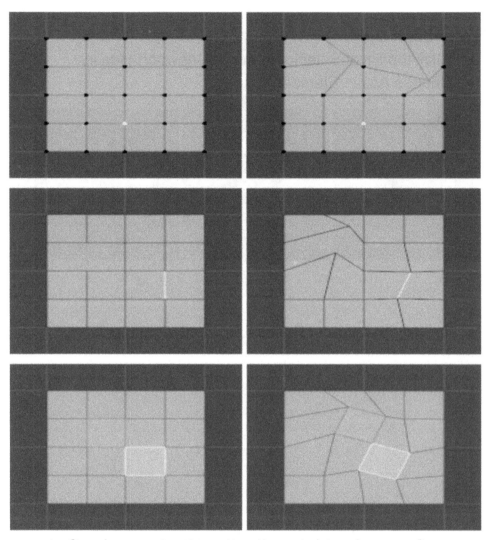

Left column: starting situation, right column: after rotation.

When to Use It:

- When aligning objects or elements to a specific reference point.
- In rigging or animation, when rotating bones around a key joint.
- When performing **precise transformations** in mechanical modeling or character design.

How to Maintain It:
- Ensure the targeted **active element** remains **last selected**. Deselect all and re-deselect in sequence if need arises.
- With **Alt + A,** delete all the selection objects and reset a new one.

Selecting the Right Pivot for Your Workflow

Understanding and application of pivot points in Blender **enhance efficiency and accuracy** during modeling, animation, or object alteration.

- Use Bounding Box Center for group transformations.
- Use **3D Cursor** for precise custom pivots.
- Use **Individual Origins** for single object transformations.
- Use **Median Point** for symmetrical modifications.
- Use **Active Element** when working with a **specific reference object.**

Practicing these types of pivots will **provide you with additional control over object manipulation,** yielding **more fluid, more accurate, and faster** workflow operation in Blender.

Exploring the Snapping Feathers in Blender 4.4

The **Snapping** feature in Blender allows for easier alignment of objects and elements in your 3D space. Whether modeling, animating, or rigging, snapping guarantees transformations to be accurate and efficient.

How to Enable Snapping

Snapping may be turned on by tapping the **magnet icon** in the 3D Viewport header. For quick, temporary access to snapping when you are editing an object, simply press **Ctrl**.

Shortcut: To turn snapping on and off quickly, press **Shift + Tab.**

Snap Base

The **Snap Base** controls which part of the item you choose to snap will be snapped to the destination. It's crucial if you want fine alignment control.

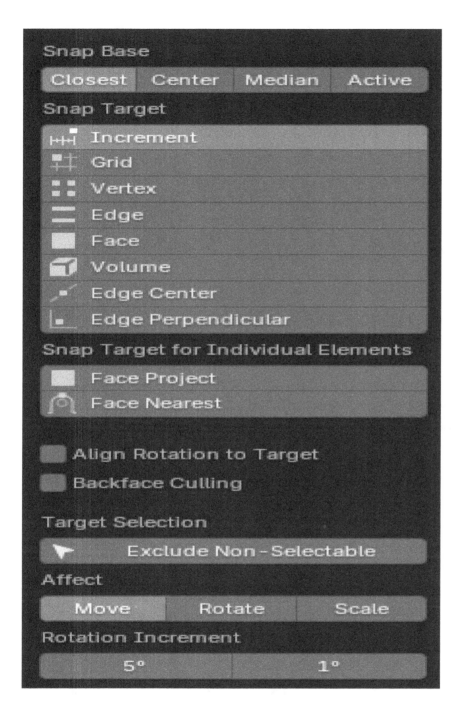

Shortcut: To bring up Snap Base settings, use **Shift + Ctrl + Tab**.

Snap Base Options

1. **Active** – Snaps to the origin of the object (in Object Mode) or to the center point of the selected element (in Edit Mode).

2. **Median** – Snaps by the **median** of the selected elements.

3. **Center** – Utilizes the transformation center (or pivot point) for snapping. This is helpful when paired with the **3D Cursor,** enabling manual snap location control.

4. **Closest** – Snaps based on the **vertex closest** to the target.

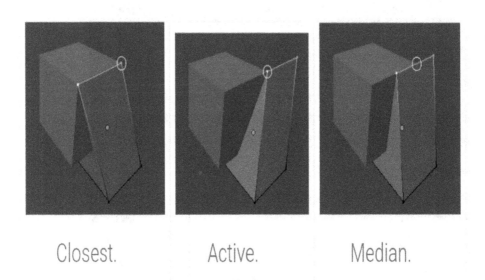

Closest.   Active.   Median.

Selecting a Snap Target

The **Snap Target** specifies where your chosen object or element will snap.

> Shortcut: Press **Shift + Ctrl + Tab** to access Snap Target settings.

Snap Target Options

1. **Increment** – Aligns objects to an **imaginary grid,** making it easy to move them in precise steps. The grid resolution adjusts based on the zoom level in Orthographic view.
2. **Grid** – Snaps directly to the visible **viewport grid.**
3. **Vertex** – Snaps to the nearest **vertex.**
4. **Edge** – Snaps to the closest **edge**.
5. **Volume** – Aligns the selection to the depth of the object at the cursor, useful for placing armature bones inside a character.
6. **Edge Center** – Snaps to the **midpoint** of the closest edge.
7. **Edge Perpendicular** – Snaps to a point on an edge in such a way that the motion is perpendicular to it.

Tip: To activate more than one snapping mode simultaneously, press **Shift** and click on them.

Snapping for Individual Elements

When you are working with lots of objects or elements, you can specify how individual pieces snap.

Snap Methods for Individual Elements
- **Face Project** – Snaps to the **face** at the cursor position, great for projecting a flat object onto a curved surface (such as the **Shrinkwrap Modifier).**
- **Face Nearest** – Snaps all objects or vertices to the nearest face, even if it's hidden under other geometry.

Advanced Snapping Options

There are some additional settings Blender provides to get extremely particular about how snapping is done:

- **Include Active Edit Mode** – Snaps to the elements of the active object.
- **Include Edited Edit Mode** – Snaps to other objects in Edit Mode.
- **Include Non-Edited Edit Mode** – Snaps to objects that are not in Edit Mode.
- **Exclude Non-Selectable** – Does not snap to non-selectable objects.
- **Align Rotation to Target** – Aligns the **Z-axis** of the selection with the target's normal.
- **Backface Culling** – Omit back-facing geometry during snapping.
- **Snap to Same Target (Face Nearest)** – Makes the object snap into the same object that it was closest to at the start of the transformation.
- **Face Nearest Steps** – Breaks down the transformation into many steps to make more uniform snapping.
- **Snap Peel Object Volume** – Considers multiple disjointed components of an object as a single volume to snap to.

Adjusting Snapping Behavior

You are able to choose whether snapping is used for movement, rotation, or scaling.

- **Rotation Increment** – Toggles the angle increments of the rotation snapping.
- **Precision Rotation** – Allows more accurate rotation when pressing down **Shift.**

Blender snapping tools mastered help optimize workflow, and modeling and transformations are more precise. From aligning objects to a grid to snapping to vertices, and from optimizing mesh placement, these tools bring precision and speed.

CHAPTER 19:

PROPORTIONAL EDITING IN BLENDER 4.4:

Blender's **Proportional Editing** feature allows you to distort selected objects and, simultaneously, influence neighboring unselected objects. The farther away you go from the selected object, the smaller the influence becomes, hence achieving smooth deformations, especially for intricate meshes.

Proportional Editing popover.

Shortcut: Press **O** to turn Proportional Editing on or off.

Understanding Proportional Editing

This tool is useful during the formation of organic deforms, such as changing facial features in character modeling or forming terrain shapes. Instead of modifying the selected vertex, Proportional Editing goes an extra step by extending its effects onto neighboring vertices with a predefined radius, creating a smoother effect.

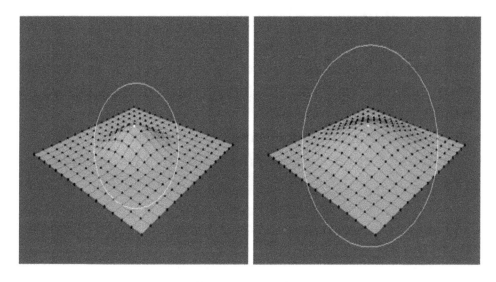

Influence circle.

Sculpting Alternative

Whereas Proportional Editing provides smooth transitions, there is also Blender's **Sculpting** system that can be used with advanced brushes which may warp meshes without the need to select certain vertices directly.

Activating and Setting Proportional Editing

On and Off
- **Off (O)** – Only selected vertices will change.
- **On (O)** – Neighbor vertices also will be affected within a radius defined.

Altering the Influence Radius

You can alter the impact of the tool by increasing or decreasing its **influence radius**. You can do this in real time while you are transforming objects:
- **Increase Radius** – Scroll **Wheel Up** or Page Up.
- **Decrease Radius** – Scroll **Wheel Down** or **Page Down.**

> As you adjust the radius, surrounding points will adjust dynamically, reacting to the transformation.

Proportional Falloff Customization

Proportional Editing allows you to control how the transformation diminishes with distance by selecting different **falloff** profiles.

Shortcut: Press **Shift + O** to open the falloff selection menu.

Falloff Types

Each falloff type determines how smoothly the transformation tapers off:

1. **Constant** – No falloff; all the deformed elements move in a constant fashion.
2. **Random** – Introduces randomness and is well suited for creating rough terrain.
3. **Linear** – Creates a linear, straight transition.
4. **Sharp** – Strong force close to the selection but decreases quickly.
5. **Root** – Smooth transition, suitable for minor deformations.
6. **Sphere** – Creates an effect close to a spherical gradient.
7. **Smooth** – Creates a smooth, natural deformation.
8. **Inverse Square** – Exerts tremendous influence near the selection but falls off quickly at a squared rate.

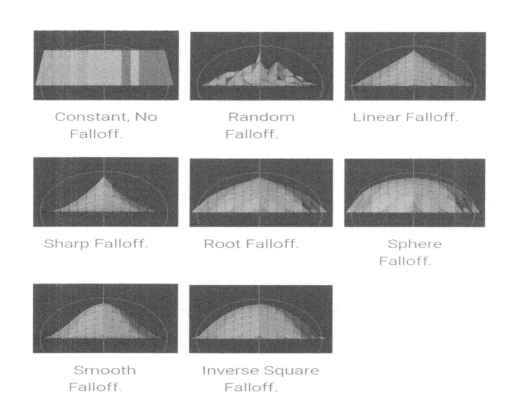

Constant, No Falloff.

Random Falloff.

Linear Falloff.

Sharp Falloff.

Root Falloff.

Sphere Falloff.

Smooth Falloff.

Inverse Square Falloff.

All of these types of falloff give you different levels of control based on what you're modeling.

Using Proportional Editing in Different Modes

Object Mode

Though applied primarily in Edit Mode, **Proportional Editing** is also available to be used in **Object Mode,** but this time on entire objects rather than vertices.

Example: When you scale a cylinder while in Object Mode, objects around it will also scale based on proportional radius, creating a smooth interaction between objects.

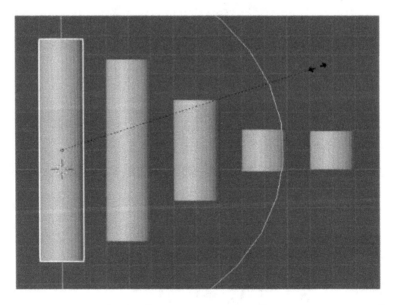

Proportional Editing in Object Mode.

Edit Mode

In **Edit Mode**, Proportional Editing is ideal for modifying dense meshes while maintaining a smooth surface. It prevents sudden lumps or irregularities in the geometry when making adjustments.

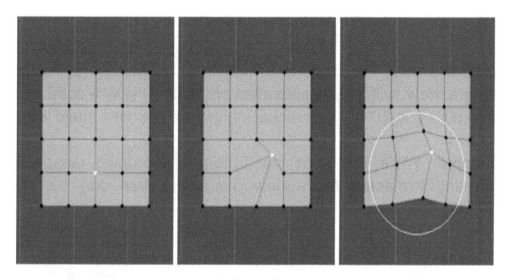

Proportional Editing in Edit Mode.

Advanced Proportional Editing Options

Connected Only (Alt + O)

Since its name suggests, Proportional Editing modifies encircling features in a place, automatically or otherwise independent of whether the features have connected shared geometry. However, choosing

Connected Only ensures the modification spreads through means of geometry which has been specifically connected only.

Example: When you're editing a finger on a character's hand, if you enable **Connected Only**, it will only affect that finger, without affecting the others—even though they might be near each other in 3D space.

Projected from View

When activated, the proportional radius only operates in the local **camera view**, without consideration of depth. This is a good option when editing in **2D-style** or reshaping geometry from a static view.

Example: While editing a mesh from a top-down perspective, activating **Projected from View** guarantees that only the items viewable from there are affected.

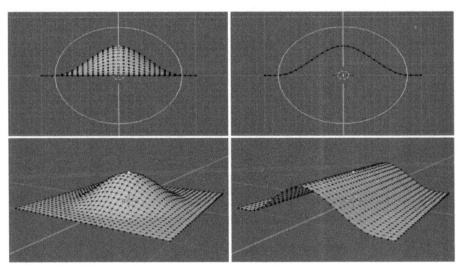

The difference between having «Projected from View» disabled (left) and enabled (right).

Practical Example:

Creating a Low-Poly Landscape

One of the best uses for Proportional Editing is building natural shapes like landscapes. Simply select vertices on a triangulated grid and nudge them upward with Proportional Editing activated, and you can build a natural mountain chain with rounded hills and valleys.

A landscape obtained via Proportional Editing.

Proportional Editing is an essential tool for any Blender user looking to make smooth, natural deformations. Whether you're sculpting a character, designing terrains, or making minor adjustments to a complex model, mastering this feature will greatly enhance your workflow.

CHAPTER 20

ADVANCED TROUBLESHOOTING TECHNIQUES IN BLENDER 4.4

Blender is an extremely powerful and feature-packed 3D tool, but being such a complicated instrument, at times it also throws some troubles its way. Be it a crash, slowness, rendering issues, or other kind of unexpected action, this advanced troubleshooting manual delivers step-by-step solutions to every possible issue found in Blender 4.4.

Blender Crashes or Freezes

Possible Causes:
- Lack of system resources (RAM, GPU, or CPU overloading).
- Outdated or incompatible graphics drivers.
- Add-ons in conflict or damaged Blender settings.
- Instability or bugs in experimental functionality.

Solutions:
A. Check System Requirements & Resource Usage
- Ensure your system has the minimum recommended specs for Blender.
- Open Task Manager (Windows) or Activity Monitor (Mac) to check RAM and CPU usage.
- Close background programs consuming memory or CPU.

B. Update Graphics Drivers

Windows Users:

- **Open Device Manager** → Locate **Display Adapters** → Right-click on your graphics card → Choose **Update Driver.**
- Or download the latest drivers directly from NVIDIA, AMD, or Intel's websites.

Mac Users:

- Ensure that macOS is up to date as Apple automatically does GPU driver updates.

C. Reset Blender Preferences

- Open Blender and navigate to **Edit > Preferences > Load Factory Settings.**
- Reboot Blender and see if the issue still persists.
- In case Blender doesn't open, remove the **preferences folder** manually:

  - **Windows**: `C:\\Users\\YourUserName\\AppData\\Roaming\\Blender Foundation\\Blender\\4.4\\config\\`
  - **Mac:** `~/Library/Application Support/Blender/4.4/config/`
  - **Linux:** `~/.config/blender/4.4/config/`

D. Turn off Add-ons & Scripts

- Third-party add-ons are sometimes the culprit that makes Blender crash.
- Start Blender in **Safe Mode:**
- Start Blender using the `--factory-startup` command in the terminal or command prompt.
- If Blender loads normally, turn off all add-ons in **Edit > Preferences > Add-ons** and turn them on one at a time to identify the culprit.

Slow Viewport Performance

Possible Causes:
- High-poly scenes.
- Big texture files taking up GPU memory.
- Inadequately optimized lighting and shading options.

Solutions:
A. Optimize Geometry & Meshes
- Apply **Decimate Modifier** to minimize polycount whenever possible.
- While in **Edit Mode,** delete excess vertices using **Merge by Distance** (shortcut **M**).
- Utilize **instancing** rather than object duplication to minimize performance lag.

B. Adjust Viewport Settings
- Switch to **Wireframe Mode** (Z → Wireframe) in order to speed up navigation.
- Minimize viewport overlays (**Viewport Overlays > Disable Extras**).
- Reduce subdivision levels in **Modifiers > Subdivision Surface.**

C. Get GPU Acceleration to work
- Navigate to **Edit > Preferences > System** and select your GPU in **Cycles Render Devices.**
- Use **Eevee** in place of **Cycles** if real-time is paramount.
- Lower **Shadow Cube Size** and **Reflection Cubemap Size** in **Render Properties > Eevee Settings.**

Rendering Takes Too Long

Possible Causes:
- High sample count in Cycles renderer.
- Inefficient light bounces increasing render times.
- Large textures consuming excessive memory.

Solutions:
A. Optimize Render Settings
- Reduce **Samples** in **Render Properties > Sampling.**
- Use **Adaptive Sampling** so that Blender can automatically scale the samples per pixel.
- Enable **Denoising** (OptiX for NVIDIA GPUs, Intel Open Image Denoise for CPUs).
- Reduce **Max Bounces** in **Render Properties > Light Paths.**

B. Optimize Textures
- Use **compressed** or **lower-res** textures where possible.
- Compress large image textures to **JPEG or WebP** instead of PNG.
- Enable **Texture Optimization** from **Edit > Preferences > System.**

C. Use GPU Instead of CPU Rendering
- If in **Cycles**, use **GPU Compute** instead of CPU.
- If your GPU supports **OptiX or CUDA,** utilize them for faster rendering.

Objects Appear Black or Have No Textures

Possible Reasons:
- Missing texture files or broken texture links.

- Shading setup in the **Shader Editor** is incorrect.
- Normals are reversed, leading to incorrect shading.

Solutions:
A. Check Texture Paths
- Navigate to **File > External Data > Find Missing Files** and choose the directory where your textures reside.
- Use **Pack Resources** to pack textures into the `.blend` file directly.

B. Fix Flipped Normals
- Enter **Edit Mode** (Tab) → Select all vertices (A) → **Shift + N** to recompute normals.
- If the issue persists, enable **Face Orientation** in **Viewport Overlays** to check flipped faces.

C. Check Shader Settings
- Enter the **Shader Editor** and ensure textures are correctly linked.
- Use **Principled BSDF** for realistic physical materials.

Unexpected Artifacts or Glitches in Renders

Possible Causes:
- Overlapping faces or intersecting geometry.
- Incorrect shadow settings or light bounces.
- Transparency or refraction issues in glass materials.

Solutions:
A. Remove Overlapping Geometry
- In Edit Mode, select the entire mesh (A) → **Merge by Distance (M)** to remove duplicates.

- Choose interior faces through **Select > Select Interior Faces** and delete them.

B. Tune Shadow & Lighting Settings
- When rendering with **Eevee**, increase **Shadow Resolution** in **Render Properties.**
- For **Cycles,** reduce noise through Denoising under the **Render Properties** tab.

C. Repair Transparency & Glass Artifacts
- When with **Eevee**, enable **Screen Space Reflections** and **Refraction** in **Render Properties.**
- In **Shader Editor,** set the **Blend Mode** to **Alpha Blend** under **Material Properties > Settings.**

6. Blender Won't Open or Crashes on Startup

Possible Causes:
- Corrupted startup file or user preferences.
- Outdated graphics drivers or incompatible GPU.
- Incompatible add-ons that won't allow Blender to start.

Solutions:
A. Start Blender with Factory Settings
- Launch Blender using the `--factory-startup` command in **Command Prompt** (Windows) or **Terminal** (Mac/Linux).
- If Blender starts up successfully, reset preferences and turn off all add-ons.

B. Check Crash Logs
- Open **Blender's Crash Log:**

- **Windows:**
  `C:\\Users\\YourUserName\\AppData\\Local\\Temp\\blender.crash.txt`
- **Mac/Linux:** `~/.config/blender/4.4/crash/`

Solution: Review error messages to identify the cause of the crash.

C. Update or Reinstall Blender
- Download the latest Blender version from **[Blender's official site](https://www.blender.org/download/.**
- If issues persist, try installing **Blender LTS (Long-Term Support)** for stability.

Blender is such a powerful application, but like any advanced piece of software, there is need for troubleshooting so that it functions smoothly. Awareness of these areas of troubleshooting and their workarounds will prepare you to better deal with the unexpected problems that may arise as well as to keep your work flow uninterrupted.

If issues still persist, attempt to request help from Blender's **official forums, Stack Exchange,** or the **Blender Discord community.**

CONCLUSION

As we come to the conclusion of this comprehensive guide to **Blender 2025**, it's a good moment to reflect on how far we've traveled. By following this book, you've been taken on a comprehensive tour of Blender's powerful features, workflows, and best practices, equipping you with the know-how required to produce stunning 3D projects—whether in modeling, sculpting, animation, rendering, or visual effects.

The Evolution of Blender: An Unrestricted Tool

Blender has evolved quite a bit over the years since its creation, with **Blender 2025** securing its place as a go-to tool for the 3D artist, the animator, the game developer, and the film director. From groundbreaking improvements in **real-time rendering, artificial intelligence-driven workflows, physics simulation, and procedural geometry,** Blender continues to blur the lines on what can and cannot be accomplished in 3D content development.

Unlike other proprietary software, Blender stands out due to its **open-source nature,** and it survives on a passionate global community of developers, artists, and hobbyists. This means that Blender can only continue to improve with unlimited opportunity for creativity and innovation.

Key Takeaways: What You've Learned

Throughout this book, we have discussed:

1. **Getting Started with Blender** – Installation, setup, and an overview of Blender's interface and major shortcuts.
2. **Modeling & Sculpting** – Techniques for developing basic or advanced 3D models using modifiers, mesh tools, and sculpt brushes.
3. **Materials & Texturing** – Proficiency in **PBR (Physically-Based Rendering)** workflows, texture mapping, and shader nodes to animate models.
4. **Lighting & Rendering** – Utilizing **Cycles, Eevee, and AI rendering** to produce photorealistic or stylized appearance.
5. **Animation & Rigging** – Rigging and animating characters and objects with the use of **keyframe animation, inverse kinematics, motion capture, and complex rigging techniques.**
6. **Physics & Simulations** – Simulating real-world effects by utilizing **fluid, cloth, soft body, and rigid body dynamics.**
7. **Compositing & Post-Processing** – Enhancing renders with the utilization of Blender's **Compositor, color grading tools, and motion tracking abilities.**
8. **Video Editing & Motion Graphics** – Using Blender's **Video Sequence Editor (VSE)** for high-quality video production.
9. **Troubleshooting & Optimization** – Debugging common problems, improving viewport performance, and optimizing render times for speed.

Blender as a Career & Creative Tool

Learning Blender isn't learning a software—it's opening career doors in 3D design, animation, game development, VFX, architecture, and even AI-generated content. Blender is now widely used in professional studios, indie game development, and Hollywood blockbusters. With its growing industry applications, learning Blender can become a significant career booster.

The Journey Never Ends: Keep Learning, Keep Creating

Although this book has been a linear method of learning Blender, **practice and experimentation are the key to true mastery.** The 3D design world is constantly evolving, and the active Blender community has unlimited resources, tutorials, and support at their fingertips.

What's Next?
- **Join the Blender Community** – Participate in forums, Discord channels, and Blender Stack Exchange to learn from other artists.
- **Take up New Challenges** – Start independent projects, contribute to open-source films, or participate in Blender-based competitions.
- **Get Updated on New Features** – Each new version of Blender has a punch. Follow **Blender's official website** and keep updated regularly.
- **Experiment & Innovate** – Explore the limits of what Blender can do by trying out **AI-assisted modeling, procedural generation, VR content creation, and simulation-based art.**

Blender is not software—it's a gateway to **bringing imagination to life.** Whatever your dream is—to create breathtaking animations, craft immersive game worlds, or produce breathtaking visual effects, **you now possess the tools to bring it to life**.

Your Blender journey doesn't stop here—it's about to begin. Keep breaking boundaries, honing your skills, and above all, **have fun creating.**

Happy Blending! God bless you

INDEX